▼▼▼▼▼▼▼▼▼▼▼▼▼▼▼▼▼▼

THE NEW EBONY COOKBOOK

THE NEW EBONY COOKBOOK

By Charlotte Lyons

JOHNSON PUBLISHING COMPANY

CHICAGO, NEW YORK, WASHINGTON, D.C., LOS ANGELES, LONDON, PARIS, JOHANNESBURG, S.A.

Johnson Publishing Company, Inc.
820 S. Michigan Avenue, Chicago, IL 60605

Library of Congress Cataloging-in-Publication Data

Lyons, Charlotte, 1950-
    The New Ebony Cookbook/by Ebony food editor, Charlotte Lyons.
        p. cm.
    ISBN 0-87485-090-8 (hb : alk. paper)
        1. Cookery, American. 2. Afro-American cookery. I. Title.

    TX715 .L969 1999
    641.5--dc21   99-049232

The *New **Ebony** Cookbook* is not a revised or updated version of
The Ebony Cookbook, first published as a *Date with a Dish*, 1948 (c), 1962, 1973.

Book Design: Ute Jansen Alonzo
Photography: James Mitchell

Manufactured By:
Quebecor World Versailles
Y 10 09 08 07
P 11 10 9 8
Printed In The United States Of America

ACKNOWLEDGEMENTS

▼ ▼

I would like to thank Linda Johnson Rice and Mr. and Mrs. John H. Johnson for giving me the opportunity to do this book. Without them, this book would not be possible. I would also like to thank my mother and son for their support and inspiration.

CONTENTS

▼ ▼

INTRODUCTION

▼ ▼ ▼ ▼ ▼ ▼ ▼ ▼ ▼ ▼ ▼ ▼ ▼ ▼ ▼ ▼ ▼ ▼ ▼ ▼

Since my early childhood, I have had a keen interest in cooking, and I loved being in the kitchen with my mother and grandmother, both of whom were excellent cooks. Some of my most memorable times were spent in the kitchen, particularly in my mother's kitchen during holidays and special occasions. Sometimes I would help with the food preparation—shelling peas, stringing beans, shucking corn, etc. I was happy to help in any way that I could, and I eventually became a pretty good cook myself.

As I grew older, my interest in cooking escalated, and I later received a bachelor of science degree in home economics from Morris Brown College in Atlanta, Georgia. The thing I have enjoyed is creating new recipes and adding my special touch to old ones. I have also gotten great pleasure out of garnishing food and making it appealing and appetizing. To this day, my friends love coming to my house for dinner because I always have something new and different for them to try.

As I look back, I realize that I have been truly blessed because each job that I have had involved working with food in some way and led to my current position as Food Editor for EBONY magazine. In my first job, I was employed by Atlanta Gas Light Company, where I was responsible for recipe development and cooking demonstrations. Later, I moved to New Jersey to take a position with Campbell Soup Company, which hired me to do recipe development, food styling and some new product development.

I wanted to gain more experience in food styling, so I took a job with General Mills in Minneapolis, Minnesota, and worked in the Betty Crocker Test Kitchen. While at General Mills, I gained extensive experience in food styling for film and print. Later I used that experience to style food for cookbooks, magazine ads, television ads and product packages.

After 4½-year stint at General Mills, I received a mailgram from Johnson Publishing Company, concerning the position of Food Editor for EBONY. I was blessed with this position, which since 1985 has enabled me to use all of the skills that I have acquired.

Working on this cookbook has been a dream come true for me. It contains some of my favorite recipes and some of the most popular ones that have appeared in EBONY. This book includes a wonderful collection of contemporary and traditional recipes that are suitable for most occasions. I have also included a section on timely tips, which allows me to share the knowledge I have gained about food over the years.

I hope you enjoy using this cookbook as much as I have enjoyed writing it.

Charlotte Lyons

APPETIZERS

Coconut Shrimp

Coconut Shrimp

1	POUND FRESH OR FROZEN RAW SHRIMP IN SHELLS
	VEGETABLE OIL
1/2	CUP ALL-PURPOSE FLOUR
1/2	TEASPOON SALT
1/8	TEASPOON WHITE PEPPER
3	EGG WHITES
1 1/2	CUPS SHREDDED COCONUT

Peel shrimp, leaving tails intact. If shrimp is frozen, do not thaw; peel under running cold water. Make a shallow cut lengthwise down back of each shrimp; wash out vein.

Heat oil (about 2 to 3 inches) in deep fryer or Dutch oven to 325 degrees. Combine flour, salt and pepper. Beat egg whites just until foamy. Coat shrimp with flour mixture; dip into beaten egg whites. Pat coconut onto shrimp, covering completely. Fry shrimp, turning once, until coconut is golden brown, about 2 minutes; drain.

Yields 4 servings

Shrimp-Filled Deviled Eggs

6	HARD-BOILED EGGS
1/4	CUP SANDWICH SPREAD
1	TEASPOON PREPARED MUSTARD
	DASH HOT PEPPER SAUCE
	SALT TO TASTE
6	MEDIUM SHRIMP, COOKED AND FINELY CHOPPED
1	GREEN ONION, FINELY CHOPPED

Cut peeled eggs lengthwise into halves. Slip out yolks; mash with fork. Mix in sandwich spread, mustard, hot pepper sauce and salt. Stir in shrimp and green onion. Fill whites with egg yolk mixture, heaping it lightly. A pastry bag can be used to fill egg whites. Arrange on large plate. Cover and chill. Garnish with paprika if desired.

Yields 12 deviled eggs

Tequila Chicken Wings

2 1/2	POUNDS CHICKEN WINGS
1/4	CUP TEQUILA
1/4	CUP FRESH LIME JUICE
1/3	CUP OLIVE OIL
2	TABLESPOONS CHILI POWDER
1	TEASPOON SUGAR
1/4	TEASPOON SALT, OPTIONAL

Cut wings in half at joint; remove wing tip and discard. Combine tequila, lime juice, olive oil, chili powder, sugar and salt in small bowl. Place chicken wings in glass shallow dish and pour marinade over wings. Cover with plastic wrap and marinate in refrigerator for one hour or longer.

Place wings on greased broiler rack in foil-lined broiler pan. Place broiler pan so that chicken wings are 5 to 7 inches from heat. Broil and cook 12 to 15 minutes, turning frequently and brushing with marinade as wings cook. Serve with hot sauce or spicy tomato salsa.

Yields 6 servings

Orange-Barbecued Chicken Wings

2 1/2 TO 3 POUNDS CHICKEN WINGS
    SALT AND PEPPER TO TASTE
1   18-OUNCE BOTTLE BARBECUE SAUCE
3/4   CUP FRESH ORANGE JUICE
1   TEASPOON WORCESTERSHIRE SAUCE
1   TEASPOON GRATED ORANGE RIND
1/8 TO 1/4 TEASPOON GROUND CLOVES
1   CLOVE GARLIC, CRUSHED

Split chicken wings at each joint and discard tips; pat dry. Season wings with salt and pepper. Place wings on broiler pan. Bake at 400 degrees for 25 to 30 minutes or until done.

Combine barbecue sauce, orange juice, Worcestershire sauce, rind, cloves and garlic in saucepan. Heat to boiling; reduce heat and simmer for 5 minutes, stirring occasionally. Brush sauce over wings.

Yields 8 servings

Ginger-Garlic Chicken Wings

1/4   CUP SOY SAUCE
1/3   CUP CHICKEN BROTH
1/4   CUP FINELY CHOPPED GINGERROOT
4   CLOVES GARLIC, FINELY CHOPPED
4   TEASPOONS DARK SESAME OIL
1   TEASPOON BROWN SUGAR
1   TEASPOON RICE VINEGAR
1/8   TEASPOON CAYENNE
3   POUNDS CHICKEN WING DRUMMETTES

VEGETABLE COOKING SPRAY

Combine all ingredients except chicken wings and vegetable cooking spray in glass baking dish. Add drummettes, turning to coat; cover and refrigerate 2 hours, turning occasionally. Remove from marinade. Spray broiler pan with vegetable cooking spray. Arrange wings on broiler pan. Broil 5 to 6 inches from heat, about 7 minutes on each side or until done, turning once.

Yields 6 servings

Buffalo Chicken Wings

3   POUNDS CHICKEN WINGS
    VEGETABLE OIL
1/4   CUP BUTTER OR MARGARINE
1/3   CUP HOT PEPPER SAUCE
1   TABLESPOON FRESH LEMON JUICE
1   TABLESPOON HONEY
    BLUE CHEESE DRESSING

Wash wings, split at each joint and discard tips. Deep fry wings in oil at 400 degrees for 10 to 15 minutes or bake in 400-degree oven for 25 minutes until crispy. Drain well. Melt butter; stir in hot sauce, lemon juice and honey. Dip wings in sauce. Serve with celery sticks and Blue Cheese dressing.

Yields 6 to 8 servings

Easy Guacamole

3	RIPE AVOCADOS, PEELED
1	SMALL ONION, FINELY CHOPPED
3	TABLESPOONS FRESH LIME OR LEMON JUICE
1	JALAPEÑO PEPPER, SEEDED AND FINELY CHOPPED, OPTIONAL
1	TEASPOON SEASONING SALT
1	LARGE TOMATO, SEEDED AND DICED
	TORTILLA OR CORN CHIPS

Halve the avocados, remove the pits and scoop out the pulp with a spoon into a medium-size non-aluminum bowl. Mash the pulp coarsely with fork. Add onion, lime juice, jalapeño, seasoning salt and tomato. Gently stir to combine ingredients. Serve with tortilla or corn chips.

Yields about 3 cups of dip

Easy Shrimp Dip

1	8-OUNCE PACKAGE CREAM CHEESE, SOFTENED
1/2	CUP MAYONNAISE
1/2	POUND SHRIMP, COOKED AND CHOPPED
4	GREEN ONIONS, THINLY SLICED
1/2	CUP WATER CHESTNUTS, CHOPPED
2	TABLESPOONS FRESH LEMON JUICE
	HOT PEPPER SAUCE TO TASTE

Combine cream cheese and mayonnaise in mixing bowl. Add remaining ingredients and mix until well-blended. Chill. Serve with crackers or fresh vegetables.

Yields about 2 cups

Double Onion Dip

1	16-OUNCE CONTAINER SOUR CREAM
1	ENVELOPE ONION SOUP MIX
1/2	SMALL RED ONION, FINELY CHOPPED
	DASH HOT PEPPER SAUCE

Mix together sour cream, soup mix, onion and hot pepper sauce in small bowl until well-blended. Chill.

Yields about 2 cups

Spinach Dip

2	10-OUNCE PACKAGES FROZEN CHOPPED SPINACH, THAWED AND DRAINED WELL
1	8-OUNCE CAN WATER CHESTNUTS, DRAINED AND FINELY CHOPPED
2	CUPS DAIRY SOUR CREAM
1/4	CUP FINELY CHOPPED GREEN ONIONS
1	TEASPOON SALT
1/4	TEASPOON DRY MUSTARD
1/4	TEASPOON PEPPER
1	CLOVE GARLIC, MINCED

Mix all ingredients together. Cover and refrigerate 1 hour. Serve with raw vegetables or potato chips.

Yields 3½ cups

Brie En Croute

1   EGG YOLK, BEATEN
1   TABLESPOON WATER
1   SHEET COMMERCIAL PUFF PASTRY, THAWED
1   8-OUNCE BRIE OR CAMEMBERT CHEESE, WITH
      RIND INTACT

Heat oven to 400 degrees. Beat egg yolk with 1 tablespoon water. Divide pastry sheet into halves. Roll out 1 pastry half until approximately 1/2-inch larger than the circle of cheese. Place cheese in center of circle. Brush edges with egg mixture. Roll second half of pastry until it is large enough to fit over the cheese. Place over cheese and press edges to seal, crimping carefully. Cut excess pastry into strips and decorate the top. Brush top and sides with egg mixture and place encased cheese on ungreased baking sheet. Bake for 20 minutes or until the pastry is puffy and brown. Cut in wedges and serve at room temperature.

Yields 1 Brie En Croute

Spicy Catfish Fingers

1   POUND CATFISH FILLETS
1/2   TEASPOON GARLIC POWDER
1/8 TO 1/4 TEASPOON CAYENNE
      SALT TO TASTE
3/4   CUP CORNMEAL
1/4   CUP ALL-PURPOSE FLOUR
1/2   TEASPOON PAPRIKA
      VEGETABLE OIL

Cut fillets into strips; set aside. Combine garlic powder, cayenne and salt; sprinkle a little on both sides of fish. Let stand a few minutes. Combine cornmeal, flour and paprika. Coat fish strips with cornmeal mixture. Pour oil to a depth of 1½ inches in heavy skillet. Fry about one-fourth of fish strips in hot oil (about 375 degrees) over medium high heat, about 2 to 3 minutes or until done and golden. Remove and drain on paper towel; set aside. Repeat with remaining fish strips. Serve with tartar sauce if desired.

Yields about 6 servings

Sardine Spread

2   3¾-OUNCE CANS NORWAY SARDINES
      IN OIL, DRAINED
1   8-OUNCE PACKAGE LIGHT CREAM CHEESE, SOFTENED
1/2   CUP CHOPPED CELERY
1/4   CUP CHOPPED RED ONION
3   TABLESPOONS CHOPPED FRESH DILL OR 1 TABLESPOON
      DRIED DILL WEED
3   TABLESPOONS PREPARED HORSERADISH
1   TABLESPOON PREPARED YELLOW MUSTARD
      DASH SALT
      DASH HOT PEPPER SAUCE
      RED OR GREEN BELL PEPPER, HALVED

Combine all ingredients except red or green bell pepper with a fork, blend thoroughly. Serve mounded in bowl or in red and/or green bell pepper halves. Surround with crackers if desired. Can be prepared and refrigerated up to two days ahead.

Yields 2 cups

Confetti Cheese Ball

1 1/2 cups shredded sharp cheddar cheese (about 10 ounces)
1   8-ounce package cream cheese, softened
1   2½-ounce package smoked beef slices, chopped
1/4 cup thinly sliced green onions
2   tablespoons chopped pimientos
1   teaspoon Worcestershire sauce
    Dash hot pepper sauce
    Chopped parsley or chopped nuts

Combine cheddar cheese and softened cream cheese, mixing at medium speed in mixer bowl until well-blended. Add chopped beef, green onions, pimientos, Worcestershire and hot pepper sauce; mix well. Chill several hours or overnight. Shape cheese mixture into a ball. Roll in chopped parsley. Serve with crackers.

Yields 1 cheese ball

Mini Quiche

1 1/4 cups buttermilk baking mix
1/4 cup butter or margarine, softened
2   tablespoons boiling water
6   slices bacon, crisply fried and crumbled
1/2 cup half-and-half
1   egg
2   tablespoons thinly sliced green onions
1/4 teaspoon salt
    Dash hot pepper sauce
1/2 cup shredded Swiss cheese

Heat oven to 375 degrees. Generously grease 24 small muffin cups, 1¾x1 inch. Mix baking mix and butter. Add boiling water; stir vigorously until soft dough forms. Press rounded teaspoonful of dough on bottom and up side of each muffin cup.

Divide bacon evenly among muffin cups. Beat half-and-half and egg; stir in onions, salt and pepper sauce. Spoon 1½ teaspoons into each muffin cup; sprinkle cheese over top. Bake until edges are golden brown and centers are set, about 20 minutes. Refrigerate any remaining appetizers.

Yields 24 appetizers

Bruchetta

1   large ready-to-eat pizza crust
    (or similar bread)
1   tablespoon olive oil
2   cloves garlic, finely chopped
1   cup diced tomatoes
8 to 10 fresh basil leaves, sliced in
    thin strips (or 2 teaspoons dried)
    Salt and pepper to taste
1   cup shredded Mozzarella cheese

Heat oven to 375 degrees. Toss together oil, garlic, tomatoes, basil, cheese, salt and pepper in bowl. Spread tomato mixture on top of pizza crust. Place on baking sheet and bake for 8 to 10 minutes or until cheese melts. Cut into slices and serve immediately.

Yields 4 to 6 servings

Tropical Punch With Fruited Ice Ring

Tropical Punch
With Fruited Ice Ring

1	46-OUNCE CAN RED FRUIT PUNCH
1	6-OUNCE CAN FROZEN LEMONADE CONCENTRATE
1	6-OUNCE CAN FROZEN ORANGE JUICE CONCENTRATE
2	CUPS CANNED PINEAPPLE JUICE
4	CUPS WATER
1/2	CUP SUGAR
	ICE
1	28-OUNCE BOTTLE GINGER ALE, CHILLED

Combine all ingredients except ice and ginger ale. Place ice in large punch bowl; pour fruit punch mixture over ice. Carefully pour in ginger ale, stirring to mix. Garnish with fruit or ice ring if desired.

Yields 30 five-ounce servings

HOW TO MAKE ICE RING FOR PUNCH

LEMON SLICES
LIME SLICES
CHERRIES
MINT LEAVES

STEP ONE: Arrange citrus slices, mint leaves and cherries in an attractive design in ring mold.

STEP TWO: Pour water into mold to partially cover fruit; freeze. When frozen, add water to fill 3/4 full. Freeze.

STEP THREE: To unmold, quickly dip into warm water that comes just to rim of mold.

STEP FOUR: Center plate on top of mold; invert and remove mold.

NOTE: Ginger ale may be substituted for water.

Sunshine Citrus Cooler

2 1/2	CUPS COLD WATER
1	6-OUNCE CAN FROZEN ORANGE JUICE CONCENTRATE, THAWED
2	CUPS CANNED PINEAPPLE JUICE
1 1/2	CUPS VODKA
1/4	CUP LIME JUICE
1/4	CUP SUGAR
	ICE
1	12-OUNCE CAN GINGER ALE OR LEMON-LIME SODA

Combine all ingredients except ice and ginger ale in large pitcher; stir until sugar dissolves. Carefully pour in ginger ale, stirring to mix. Serve over ice if desired.

Yields about 2 quarts

Easy Frozen Daiquiri

1	6-OUNCE CAN FROZEN LIMEADE CONCENTRATE (UNDILUTED)
2 1/2	CANS LIGHT RUM (USE LIMEADE CAN TO MEASURE)
3	CANS WATER

Combine limeade, rum and water in 1½-quart freezer container; cover and freeze (mixture will not freeze solid).

Just before serving, place half of mixture in blender; cover and blend until slushy. Repeat; pour mixture into cocktail glasses.

Yields 5 cups

White Sangria

1   750 ML BOTTLE SAUTERNE
1/2   CUP SUGAR
1/4   CUP ORANGE-FLAVORED LIQUEUR
1/4   CUP FRESH LEMON JUICE
1/4   CUP FRESH LIME JUICE
1   32-OUNCE BOTTLE CLUB SODA, CHILLED
       ICE

Combine wine, sugar, orange-flavored liqueur, lemon and lime juice in large pitcher. Just before serving, add club soda. Garnish with sliced lemon, lime or strawberries if desired.

Yields 2 quarts

Frozen Piña Colada

1/4   CUP LIGHT RUM
1/4   CUP CRUSHED PINEAPPLE
3   TABLESPOONS COCONUT MILK

Place ingredients in blender with two cups of crushed ice. Blend at high speed until mixture is slushy. Pour into 2 glasses and garnish with pineapple and cherries if desired.

Yields 2 servings

Fresh Tangerine Mimosa

JUICE OF 12 MEDIUM TO LARGE TANGERINES
1   750 ML BOTTLE CHAMPAGNE, CHILLED

For each serving, pour 1/4 cup tangerine juice into tall 6-ounce champagne glass. Slowly pour in 1/4 cup champagne. Garnish with fresh mint leaves if desired.

Yields about 12 servings

Margarita

2   CUPS TEQUILA
2   CUPS TRIPLE SEC
1 1/4   CUPS FRESH LIME JUICE
         ICE
         COARSE SALT
         LIME WEDGES

Rub lime wedges around rim of glasses; dip rim in salt. Combine tequila, triple sec and lime juice in large pitcher. Add ice; stir. Serve immediately in prepared glasses.

Yields about 12 servings

Strawberry Lemonade

1 1/2   CUPS SLICED STRAWBERRIES
1   CUP FRESH LEMON JUICE (ABOUT 6 LEMONS)
1 1/2   CUPS SUGAR
4   CUPS COLD WATER

Combine strawberries, lemon juice and sugar in blender; blend until smooth. Pour strawberry mixture into a large pitcher; stir in cold water. Serve over ice. If desired, garnish with lemon slices and strawberries.

Yields about 7 cups

Champagne Punch

2   **20**-OUNCE CANS CRUSHED PINEAPPLE IN UNSWEETENED PINEAPPLE JUICE

1   **12**-OUNCE CAN FROZEN LEMONADE CONCENTRATE

1   **28**-OUNCE BOTTLE CLUB SODA, CHILLED

1   **4/5**-QUART BOTTLE CHAMPAGNE, CHILLED

Blend crushed pineapple with its liquid, one can at a time, 15 to 20 seconds until thick in covered blender. Combine blended pineapple and undiluted lemonade concentrate in large punch bowl. Stir in club soda and champagne. Add ice and serve at once.

Yields 10 servings

Banana Coconut Shake

2   MEDIUM BANANAS, SLICED

1/4   CUP CREAM OF COCONUT

2   CUPS UNSWEETENED PINEAPPLE JUICE, CHILLED

1   CUP VANILLA ICE CREAM

Combine bananas and cream of coconut in blender. Cover; blend until smooth. Add juice and ice cream. Cover; blend until smooth.

Yields 4 servings

Spiced Lemon Tea

3   CUPS BOILING WATER

6   TEA BAGS

3   CINNAMON STICKS

1/4   TEASPOON GROUND CLOVES

1/8   TEASPOON GROUND NUTMEG

2/3   CUP SUGAR

1 1/2   CUPS COLD WATER

     JUICE OF 3 LEMONS (ABOUT **1/2** CUP)

     ICE CUBES

Pour boiling water over tea bags, cinnamon sticks, cloves and nutmeg; steep 5 minutes. Remove tea bags and cinnamon sticks. Stir in sugar, cold water and lemon juice; chill. Serve over ice with cinnamon stick stirrers if desired.

Yields 5 to 6 servings

Apricot Cooler

2   CUPS APRICOT NECTAR, CHILLED

2   CUPS UNSWEETENED PINEAPPLE JUICE, CHILLED

1/3   CUP LEMON JUICE FROM CONCENTRATE

1   **12**-OUNCE CAN GINGER ALE, CHILLED

     ICE

Combine nectar, pineapple juice and lemon juice in pitcher. Just before serving, add ginger ale and serve over ice.

Yields 6 servings

SOUPS & STEWS

Easy Cassoulet

Easy Cassoulet

2   TABLESPOONS OLIVE OIL
1   POUND SMOKED OR TURKEY SAUSAGE, SLICED
4   CLOVES GARLIC, MINCED
2   STALKS CELERY, SLICED
1   MEDIUM ONION, CHOPPED
1/2 TEASPOON DRIED THYME, CRUSHED
1/2 TEASPOON DRIED ROSEMARY, CRUSHED
1   14-OUNCE CAN LOW-SALT CHICKEN BROTH
    DASH CRUSHED RED PEPPER
1   15-OUNCE CAN RED KIDNEY BEANS, DRAINED AND
    RINSED
1   15-OUNCE CAN GREAT NORTHERN BEANS, UNDRAINED
1   15-OUNCE CAN PINTO BEANS, UNDRAINED
1 TO 2 TEASPOONS BROWN SUGAR
3   GREEN ONIONS, SLICED

In large Dutch oven or heavy pot, cook sausage in oil until brown on all sides. Remove sausage. Cook garlic, celery, and onion with thyme and rosemary in the same oil until tender. Add broth, crushed red pepper and sausage. Heat to boiling; reduce heat. Cover and simmer 30 minutes. Add beans and brown sugar and cook 10 minutes longer. Garnish with sliced green onion.

Yields 8 to 10 servings

Pasta and Bean Soup

1   CUP DRIED, CLEANED CANNELLONI OR NAVY BEANS
3   LARGE CLOVES GARLIC, MINCED
1   LARGE ONION, CHOPPED
1   CUP CELERY, CHOPPED
1   MEDIUM CARROT, CHOPPED
1   TABLESPOON OLIVE OIL
3   14 ½-OUNCE CANS LOW-SALT CHICKEN BROTH
    OR VEGETABLE BROTH
2   BAY LEAVES
1   TABLESPOON DRIED OREGANO
1   TEASPOON CRACKED PEPPER
1   16-OUNCE CAN STEWED TOMATOES, UNDRAINED
1   TABLESPOON DRIED BASIL
8   OUNCES (DRY WEIGHT) PASTA (SMALL SHELLS, ZITI OR
    BOW TIES), COOKED AND DRAINED
8   OUNCES JARLSBERG LITE CHEESE, SHREDDED
    CHOPPED PARSLEY

Cover beans with 2 inches of water and soak overnight; drain beans. Cook garlic, onion, celery and carrot in oil until tender in large saucepan. Add beans, broth, bay leaves, oregano and pepper. Bring to a boil; reduce heat to simmer. Cover and continue to cook 1 hour or until beans are tender.

Add tomatoes and basil; cook 15 minutes. Add pasta and heat through. Before serving, remove bay leaves and stir in half the cheese. Serve with remaining cheese for topping.

Yields 8 to 10 servings

Cream of Broccoli Soup

2   10-OUNCE PACKAGES FROZEN CHOPPED BROCCOLI,
    THAWED
1   10¾-OUNCE CAN CHICKEN BROTH
2   SOUP CANS WATER
1   SMALL ONION, CHOPPED
1   STALK CELERY, CHOPPED
    SALT AND PEPPER
1/4 CUP ALL-PURPOSE FLOUR
2   CUPS MILK

DASH GROUND NUTMEG

SOUR CREAM OR HEAVY CREAM

Combine broccoli, broth, water, onion, celery, salt and pepper in Dutch oven. Heat to boiling; reduce heat. Cover and simmer until vegetables are tender, about 10 minutes. Pour half of vegetable mixture in food processor or blender. Blend on high speed until smooth. Repeat. Return to pan and heat until boiling. Shake flour and 1 cup milk in tightly covered container until smooth. Gradually stir into hot mixture. Boil 1 minute, stirring occasionally. Stir in remaining milk and nutmeg. Heat on low heat until hot. Garnish with sour cream or heavy cream.

Yields 6 servings

Chicken-Shrimp Gumbo Soup

1	MEDIUM ONION, CHOPPED
1	MEDIUM GREEN PEPPER, CHOPPED
1/2	CUP CELERY, SLICED
3	CLOVES GARLIC, CRUSHED
1/8	TEASPOON CRUSHED RED PEPPER
1/4	CUP BUTTER OR MARGARINE
2	TABLESPOONS ALL-PURPOSE FLOUR
3	10¾-OUNCE CANS CONDENSED CHICKEN BROTH
3	SOUP CANS WATER
1	16-OUNCE CAN WHOLE TOMATOES, UNDRAINED
1	8-OUNCE CAN WHOLE KERNEL CORN, DRAINED
1	CUP DICED COOKED CHICKEN
	HOT PEPPER SAUCE TO TASTE
1	POUND FRESH OR FROZEN RAW SHRIMP, THAWED
1	10-OUNCE PACKAGE FROZEN CUT OKRA
1/2	CUP COOKED RICE
1 TO 2	TABLESPOONS GUMBO FILÉ

Cook and stir onion, green pepper, celery, garlic and crushed red pepper in melted butter in Dutch oven over low heat until vegetables are tender. Stir in flour. Cook over low heat, stirring constantly, until bubbly; remove from heat. Stir in remaining ingredients except shrimp, okra, rice and gumbo filé; break up tomatoes with fork. Heat to boiling; reduce heat. Simmer uncovered, stirring occasionally, 15 minutes. Add shrimp, rice, and filé. Cover and simmer until shrimp are pink, about 5 minutes.

Yields 6 to 8 servings

Caramelized Onion Soup

4	TABLESPOONS BUTTER OR MARGARINE
1	LARGE ONION, COARSELY CHOPPED
2	MEDIUM LEEKS, THINLY SLICED (WHITE AND PALE GREEN PARTS ONLY)
3	LARGE SHALLOTS, THINLY SLICED
2	TABLESPOONS SUGAR
6	CUPS CHICKEN BROTH
1/4	CUP DRY WHITE WINE
	SALT AND PEPPER TO TASTE

Melt the butter in a large heavy saucepan over medium heat, and add the onion, leeks, shallots and sugar; cook and stir until onions are light golden brown, about 10 minutes. Stir in broth, wine, salt and pepper. Bring to a boil; reduce heat and simmer 20 minutes, stirring occasionally. Garnish with chopped parsley if desired.

Yields 4 servings

Black Bean Soup

1   POUND DRIED BLACK BEANS
1 1/2   CUPS CHOPPED ONION
3   CLOVES GARLIC, MINCED
1/2   CUP CHOPPED CELERY
1/2   CUP CHOPPED GREEN PEPPER
1/4   CUP OLIVE OIL
1   QUART WATER
2   13¾-OUNCE CANS BEEF BROTH
2   TEASPOONS DRIED OREGANO LEAVES
2   TEASPOONS GROUND CUMIN
1   BAY LEAF
1/4   TEASPOON PEPPER
1   TEASPOON BROWN SUGAR
1/4   CUP DRY SHERRY
    CAYENNE PEPPER TO TASTE
    SOUR CREAM
    COOKED RICE
    SLICED GREEN ONIONS

Soak beans in cold water overnight covered; drain. Cook onion, garlic, celery and green pepper in oil in Dutch oven until tender. Stir in water, broth, oregano, cumin, bay leaf, pepper, sugar, sherry, beans and cayenne pepper. Heat to boiling; reduce heat, simmer uncovered, stirring often, about 2 to 2½ hours or until beans are tender. Serve with cooked rice. Garnish with sour cream and green onions.

Yields 8 to 10 servings

Oriental Chicken Soup

3   10¾-OUNCE CANS CONDENSED CHICKEN BROTH
3   SOUP CANS WATER
2   CUPS CUBED COOKED CHICKEN
1/2   CUP CELERY, THINLY SLICED DIAGONALLY
1   MEDIUM CARROT, THINLY SLICED DIAGONALLY
1   4-OUNCE CAN MUSHROOM SLICES
1/2   CUP COOKED RICE
2   CLOVES GARLIC, MINCED
2   TABLESPOONS SOY SAUCE
1/2   TEASPOON GROUND GINGER
1   TABLESPOON DRY SHERRY
2   GREEN ONIONS, SLICED
2   OUNCES SNOW PEAS, CUT INTO STRIPS

Combine all ingredients except green onions and snow peas in Dutch oven. Bring to a boil; reduce heat and simmer 5 minutes or until vegetables are just tender. Stir in green onions and snow peas. Continue to cook for 1 to 2 minutes. Serve with additional soy sauce if desired.

Yields 6 servings

Chicken And Black-Eyed Pea Stew

1   TABLESPOON VEGETABLE OIL
3   POUNDS CHICKEN PARTS
3   CUPS CHICKEN BROTH
4   CUPS CHOPPED TOMATOES (WITH JUICE)
2   CUPS SLICED FRESH OKRA
2   CUPS FRESH OR FROZEN BLACK-EYED PEAS
1   CUP SLICED CARROTS
1   CUP FRESH OR FROZEN CORN
1   CUP CHOPPED ONION
1/2   CUP CHOPPED GREEN PEPPER
3   CLOVES GARLIC, CRUSHED
4   TEASPOONS PEPPER SAUCE
    SALT TO TASTE
1   TEASPOON DRIED THYME, CRUSHED

1	BAY LEAF
1/2	CUP ALL-PURPOSE FLOUR
3/4	CUP WATER
	HOT COOKED RICE
	SLICED GREEN ONIONS

Cook chicken parts over medium heat in oil until brown on all sides in large heavy pan or Dutch oven; spoon off fat. Add chicken broth, vegetables, garlic, pepper sauce, salt, thyme and bay leaf. Heat to boiling; reduce heat. Cover and simmer until thickest pieces of chicken are done, 15 to 20 minutes. Mix water and flour together until smooth in small bowl. Slowly add flour mixture to stew, stirring constantly to prevent lumps. Cook until mixture thickens, stirring often. Serve with rice. Garnish with green onions if desired.

Yields 6 servings

Old-Fashioned Potato Soup

4	MEDIUM POTATOES, PEELED AND DICED
2	TABLESPOONS BUTTER OR MARGARINE
1/2	CUP DICED CELERY
1/2	CUP CHOPPED ONION
3	CUPS MILK
	SALT AND PEPPER TO TASTE
	CHOPPED CHIVES

Cover potatoes with water in medium saucepan. Cover and cook until potatoes are tender, about 5 to 10 minutes. Drain potatoes. Mash half of the potatoes with a potato masher while they are still warm. Melt the butter over medium heat; add celery and onion. Cook and stir vegetables until tender, about 5 minutes. Set aside. Return potatoes to saucepan and add the celery and onion. Stir in milk, salt and pepper. Cook over medium heat, stirring frequently until smooth and hot (do not let the soup boil or it will curdle). Garnish with chives.

Yields 4 servings

Soulful Pepperpot Soup

1/2	POUND ITALIAN SAUSAGE, SLICED
1	POUND CUBED BEEF
1	TABLESPOON OIL
1	MEDIUM ONION, CHOPPED
2	CELERY STALKS, SLICED
3	CLOVES GARLIC, MINCED
3	MEDIUM TOMATOES, DICED
6	CUPS CHICKEN BROTH
4	CUPS WATER
1 1/2 TO 2	TEASPOONS GUMBO FILÉ
1	CUP CUBED COOKED CHICKEN
1/2	CUP ELBOW MACARONI
1	LARGE GREEN PEPPER, CUBED

Brown sausage and beef in oil in large heavy pan until brown on all sides. Add remaining ingredients except macaroni, chicken and green pepper. Bring to a boil; reduce heat and simmer for 1 hour, stirring occasionally. Add chicken, macaroni and green pepper and continue to cook until macaroni is done, about 7 minutes.

Yields 6 to 8 servings

▼ ▼ ▼ ▼ ▼ ▼ ▼ ▼ ▼ ▼ ▼ ▼ ▼ ▼ ▼ ▼ ▼

Beef Bourguignonne Soup

2	TABLESPOONS VEGETABLE OIL
1	POUND LEAN BONELESS BEEF CHUCK, CUT INTO 1/2-INCH CUBES
2	13¾-OUNCE CANS BEEF BROTH
1	CUP BURGUNDY WINE
1	CUP WATER
1/2	TEASPOON DRIED THYME, CRUSHED
1/2	TEASPOON DRIED MARJORAM, CRUSHED
1/4	TEASPOON PEPPER
3	CLOVES GARLIC, MINCED
2	MEDIUM CARROTS, SLICED
1/4	POUND FRESH MUSHROOMS, SLICED
1/2	POUND PEARL ONIONS, PEELED
1/4	CUP WATER
2	TABLESPOONS CORNSTARCH
2	TABLESPOONS CHOPPED PARSLEY

Heat oil in Dutch oven over medium heat. Brown beef pieces (half at a time) about 10 minutes. Pour off drippings. Add broth, wine, water, thyme, marjoram, pepper and garlic. Bring to a boil; reduce heat. Cover and simmer 1 hour and 30 minutes, stirring occasionally. Add carrots, mushrooms and onions. Continue to cook 30 more minutes. Combine water with cornstarch; gradually stir into soup. Cook uncovered about 10 minutes, stirring occasionally until thickened. Garnish with parsley.

Yields 6 to 8 servings

Garlicky Beef Stew

2	TABLESPOONS OLIVE OIL
2	TABLESPOONS ALL-PURPOSE FLOUR
1/2	TEASPOON SALT
1/4	TEASPOON PEPPER
2	POUNDS LEAN CUBED BEEF
1	WHOLE HEAD GARLIC, CUT IN HALF ACROSS THE CLOVES, PEEL LEFT ON
1	MEDIUM GREEN PEPPER, CHOPPED
3	BAY LEAVES
1	16-OUNCE CAN STEWED TOMATOES, UNDRAINED
2	CUPS BEEF BROTH
2	CUPS WATER
12	SMALL WHITE ONIONS, PEELED
4	MEDIUM POTATOES, PEELED AND QUARTERED
3	MEDIUM CARROTS, THICKLY SLICED
1/8	TEASPOON CRUSHED RED PEPPER
12	SAFFRON THREADS, FINELY CRUMBLED OR 1/2 TEASPOON TURMERIC
1	LARGE CLOVE GARLIC, CRUSHED
	SALT AND PEPPER TO TASTE
2	TABLESPOONS CHOPPED PARSLEY

Heat the oil in Dutch oven until hot over medium heat. Combine flour, salt and pepper. Coat beef with flour mixture; brown beef on all sides. Add the garlic, green pepper, bay leaves, and tomatoes; mix well. Add broth and water. Cover and simmer over low heat for 1½ hours. Add onions, potatoes, carrots, crushed red pepper, and saffron. Cover and simmer for 20 minutes, or until potatoes and carrots are tender. Add crushed garlic clove and remove bay leaves. Season with salt and pepper. Let stand 5 minutes. Sprinkle with parsley and serve.

Yields 6 servings

Chicken Corn Chowder

1	LARGE POTATO, PEELED AND DICED
1	MEDIUM CARROT, THINLY SLICED
1	MEDIUM ONION, CHOPPED
3	STALKS CELERY, THINLY SLICED
1	7-OUNCE CAN CORN, UNDRAINED
1	10¾-OUNCE CAN CONDENSED CHICKEN BROTH
2	CUPS WATER
	SALT AND PEPPER TO TASTE
1/2	CUP ALL-PURPOSE FLOUR
1	CUP MILK
1 1/2	CUPS COOKED CUT-UP CHICKEN
2	CUPS MILK
	CHOPPED PARSLEY

Add potato, carrot, onion, celery, corn, broth, water, salt and pepper in Dutch oven. Heat to boiling; reduce heat. Cover and simmer until vegetables are tender, about 10 minutes. Shake flour and 1 cup milk in tightly covered container; gradually stir into hot mixture. Heat to boiling. Boil 1 minute. Stir in chicken and remaining milk. Heat over low heat, stirring occasionally, just until hot, about 10 minutes.

Yields 6 to 8 servings

Easy Chicken Noodle Soup

3	10¾-OUNCE CANS CONDENSED CHICKEN BROTH
4	SOUP CANS WATER
2	MEDIUM CARROTS, DIAGONALLY SLICED
2	CELERY STALKS, DIAGONALLY SLICED

Chicken Vegetable Soup

1	MEDIUM ONION, CHOPPED
1	TEASPOON SEASONING SALT
1/2	TEASPOON DRIED THYME
1/8	TEASPOON PEPPER
3	CUPS COOKED CUT-UP CHICKEN
1 1/2	CUPS MEDIUM UNCOOKED NOODLES
2	GREEN ONIONS, DIAGONALLY SLICED

Heat broth, water, carrots, celery, onion and seasonings to boiling in Dutch oven; reduce heat. Cover; simmer until carrots are tender, about 15 minutes. Stir in chicken and noodles. Heat to boiling; reduce heat. Simmer uncovered 7 to 10 minutes. Stir in green onions.

Yields 8 servings

▼ ▼ ▼ ▼ ▼ ▼ ▼ ▼ ▼ ▼ ▼ ▼ ▼ ▼ ▼ ▼ ▼ ▼ ▼

Easy Lamb Vegetable Stew

1	POUND LEAN LAMB, CUT IN 3/4-INCH CUBES
2	TABLESPOONS OLIVE OIL
2	MEDIUM ONIONS, CUT INTO WEDGES
2	CLOVES GARLIC, MINCED
1/4	TEASPOON EACH DRIED THYME, BASIL, OREGANO, AND ROSEMARY
1	15-OUNCE CAN STEWED TOMATOES, UNDRAINED
3 OR 4	MEDIUM POTATOES, PEELED AND CUBED
2	CARROTS, CUT IN 1/2-INCH SLICES
2	STALKS CELERY, CUT IN 1/2-INCH SLICES
1 1/2	CUPS SMALL FRESH MUSHROOMS
1	CUP FROZEN PEAS
1	12-OUNCE JAR BROWN GRAVY

Brown lamb cubes in olive oil until browned on all sides. Add onion, garlic and herbs; mix well. Stir in stewed tomatoes, cover and simmer 15 minutes. Add potatoes, carrots, celery, and mushrooms. Cover and cook 20 to 25 minutes or until meat and vegetables are tender. Stir in peas and gravy; heat through.

Yields 4 to 6 servings

Chicken Vegetable Soup

2	TABLESPOONS BUTTER OR MARGARINE
1	MEDIUM ONION, CHOPPED
2	CELERY STALKS, SLICED
4	LEEKS, ABOUT 1 POUND, WHITE AND PALE GREEN PARTS ONLY, CLEANED AND THINLY SLICED
3	MEDIUM CARROTS, CUT INTO 1/4-INCH ROUNDS
3	POTATOES, PEELED AND CUT INTO 1/4-INCH CUBES
1/2	TEASPOON DRIED THYME
4	CUPS CHICKEN BROTH
4	CUPS WATER
	SALT AND PEPPER TO TASTE
1	POUND SKINLESS COOKED CHICKEN, CUT UP INTO 1/2-INCH PIECES
2	TABLESPOONS CHOPPED PARSLEY

Melt butter over medium heat in large saucepan; add onion, celery, leeks, carrots, potatoes and thyme. Cook and stir until onion and leeks wilt, about 5 minutes. Add chicken broth, water, salt and pepper. Cover and bring to a boil; reduce heat and simmer, uncovered for 30 minutes. Add chicken and continue to simmer for 20 to 30 minutes, skimming the surface as necessary. Garnish with parsley if desired.

Yields 4 to 6 servings

SALADS & SALAD DRESSINGS

▽▽▽▽▽▽▽▽▽▽▽▽▽▽▽▽▽▽

21

Italian Salad Bowl

Italian Salad Bowl

1   LARGE HEAD LETTUCE OR COMBINATION OF GREENS,
    WASHED AND DRAINED WELL
1   14-OUNCE CAN ARTICHOKE HEARTS, CUT INTO HALVES
2   LARGE TOMATOES, DICED
4   HARD-BOILED EGGS
1/2 CUP COARSELY CHOPPED RIPE OLIVES
1   TEASPOON SALT, OPTIONAL
1   TEASPOON PAPRIKA
2   CLOVES GARLIC, MINCED
3/4 CUP OLIVE OIL
1/4 CUP WINE VINEGAR
1   TEASPOON SUGAR

Break lettuce or greens into large salad bowl.
Arrange artichoke halves across center of bowl, rim
to rim. Place rows of tomatoes on each side of arti-
chokes. Dice egg yolks and place next to tomatoes
on one side. Dice egg whites and place next to tomatoes on the other side. Place ripe olives next to egg
whites and egg yolks. Combine salt and paprika in
jar. Add garlic, olive oil and wine vinegar. Shake
vigorously. Just before serving, pour dressing over
salad. Mix salad a section at a time so that all ingredients are blended.

Yields 8 to 10 servings

Down-Home Potato Salad

6   POTATOES, COOKED AND CUBED
4   HARD-COOKED EGGS, PEELED AND CHOPPED
1   CUP CHOPPED CELERY
1/4 CUP FINELY CHOPPED ONION

1   2-OUNCE JAR CHOPPED PIMIENTO, DRAINED
1/2 CUP SWEET PICKLE RELISH
1 1/2 CUPS MAYONNAISE OR SALAD DRESSING
2   TEASPOONS PREPARED MUSTARD
1   TEASPOON SEASONING SALT
1/4 TEASPOON PEPPER

Mix together potatoes, eggs, celery, onion,
pimiento and pickle relish in large bowl. Mix mayonnaise, mustard, seasoning salt and pepper. Pour
mayonnaise mixture over potato mixture and gently
toss potato mixture to coat. Garnish with parsley if
desired.

Yields 8 servings

Fresh Tomato Salad With Dill

2   RED TOMATOES, THICKLY SLICED
2   YELLOW TOMATOES, THICKLY SLICED
1/3 CUP VEGETABLE OIL
2   TABLESPOONS FRESH LEMON JUICE
1   TABLESPOON SNIPPED FRESH DILL WEED
1   TEASPOON SALT
1/8 TEASPOON PEPPER

Arrange tomato slices (alternate red and yellow
tomato slices) on serving platter. Combine remaining ingredients in tightly covered container and
shake until ingredients are mixed well. Spoon dressing over tomatoes. Garnish with fresh dill if desired.
Serve at once.

Yields 6 servings

Black-Eyed Pea Salad

2   10-OUNCE PACKAGES FROZEN BLACK-EYED PEAS
1   CUP BOTTLED REDUCED-CALORIE ITALIAN SALAD DRESSING
2   TEASPOONS SUGAR
1/8 TO 1/4 TEASPOON CRUSHED RED PEPPER
1/2   CUP SLICED CELERY
1/2   CHOPPED RED OR GREEN BELL PEPPER
4 TO 5 GREEN ONIONS, THINLY SLICED
1/4   CUP CHOPPED PARSLEY
    SALT AND PEPPER TO TASTE
    LETTUCE LEAVES

Cook peas as directed on package; drain. Shake Italian dressing, sugar and crushed red pepper in tightly covered container until blended. Combine cooked peas, celery, green pepper, onions and parsley. Gently toss pea mixture and salad dressing; season with salt and pepper. Chill. Serve with a slotted spoon on lettuce leaves.

Yields 6 servings

Marinated Asparagus Spears

1   POUND ASPARAGUS SPEARS, TRIMMED, COOKED, DRAINED AND CHILLED OR 1 10-OUNCE PACKAGE FROZEN ASPARAGUS
3   TABLESPOONS OLIVE OIL
3   TABLESPOONS FRESH LEMON JUICE
1   TEASPOON SUGAR
1/4   TEASPOON SALT
1/4   TEASPOON DRY MUSTARD
1/4   TEASPOON PAPRIKA
1   SMALL CLOVE GARLIC, MINCED
    SALAD GREENS

Arrange asparagus in shallow dish. Combine remaining ingredients except salad greens in jar with lid; shake well. Pour over chilled asparagus and marinate 15 to 20 minutes. Drain dressing; reserve. Arrange on salad greens. Serve with reserved dressing. Garnish with lemon slices.

Yields 4 servings

Green Beans and Herb Salad

2   POUNDS ASSORTED BEANS (SUCH AS GREEN, YELLOW AND HARICOT VERT)
6   TABLESPOONS OLIVE OIL
5   TABLESPOONS RED WINE VINEGAR
2   CLOVES GARLIC, MINCED
2   TABLESPOONS CHOPPED FRESH BASIL OR 1 TEASPOON DRIED BASIL
2   TEASPOONS CHOPPED FRESH OREGANO OR 1/2 TEA SPOON DRIED OREGANO
    SALT AND PEPPER TO TASTE

Bring a large pot filled about 3/4 full of salted water to a boil over high heat. Add beans and boil until tender, about 4 to 6 minutes. Drain and rinse under cold water to stop the cooking. Continue to cool in refrigerator for about 1 hour or more. Combine remaining ingredients in large bowl. Add cooled beans and toss well to coat beans. Garnish with chopped parsley if desired.

Yields 6 servings

Chopped Vegetable Salad

2	CELERY STALKS, DICED
2	MEDIUM CUCUMBERS, PEELED, SEEDED AND DICED
1	SMALL GREEN PEPPER, DICED
1	SMALL RED BELL PEPPER, DICED
1	SMALL YELLOW BELL PEPPER, DICED
1	SMALL RED ONION, CHOPPED
2	LARGE TOMATOES, DICED
1	TABLESPOON CANNED SLICED JALAPEÑO PEPPER, CHOPPED
1/2	CUP ITALIAN SALAD DRESSING
1	TABLESPOON FRESH LEMON JUICE
2	TABLESPOONS CHOPPED PARSLEY

Place vegetables and jalapeño in large bowl. Pour salad dressing and lemon juice over vegetables. Toss gently to coat vegetables with salad dressing. Let marinate in refrigerator for 1 hour or longer. Just before serving, stir in parsley. Spoon salad with slotted spoon onto lettuce leaves.

Yields 6 servings

Marinated Mushroom Salad

1/4	CUP OLIVE OIL
2	TABLESPOONS RICE VINEGAR
1	TEASPOON SUGAR
1	TABLESPOON CHOPPED PARSLEY
1/4	TEASPOON SALT
1/8	TEASPOON PEPPER
1	CLOVE GARLIC, FINELY MINCED
1/2	TEASPOON ITALIAN SEASONING

2	CUPS THINLY SLICED FRESH MUSHROOMS
1	LARGE TOMATO, SLICED
	LETTUCE LEAVES

Mix together olive oil, vinegar, sugar, parsley, salt and pepper, garlic and Italian seasoning in tightly covered container. Pour over mushrooms in glass or plastic bowl. Cover and refrigerate at least 4 hours but no longer than 24 hours. Arrange tomato slices on lettuce leaves. Spoon mushroom mixture on tomatoes.

Yields 4 servings

Sweet Potato Salad

4	MEDIUM SWEET POTATOES, PEELED AND COOKED
1/4	CUP PEANUT OR VEGETABLE OIL
2	TABLESPOONS FRESH LEMON JUICE
1/2	TEASPOON SALT, OPTIONAL
1/4	TEASPOON PEPPER
1/2	CUP CHOPPED CELERY
1/2	CUP CHOPPED GREEN PEPPER
1/2	CUP THINLY SLICED GREEN ONIONS
	CHOPPED PARSLEY

Cut potatoes in cubes; place in glass or plastic bowl. Mix oil, lemon juice, salt and pepper; pour over potatoes. Cover and refrigerate at least 4 hours. Stir in celery, green pepper and green onions. Garnish with chopped parsley if desired.

Yields 6 servings

Curried Chicken And Rice Salad

3	CUPS COLD COOKED RICE
2	CUPS CUT-UP COOKED CHICKEN OR TURKEY
1	CUP SLICED CELERY
1/2	CUP CHOPPED RED BELL PEPPER
1/4	CUP CHOPPED WATER CHESTNUTS
1	13¼-OUNCE CAN PINEAPPLE CHUNKS IN SYRUP, DRAINED
1	CUP MAYONNAISE OR SALAD DRESSING
1 TO 2	TEASPOONS CURRY POWDER
1	TEASPOON SUGAR
	SALT TO TASTE
	DASH CAYENNE
1/4	TEASPOON GROUND GINGER
6	SLICES BACON COOKED AND CRUMBLED (OPTIONAL)

Mix rice, chicken, celery, red bell pepper, water chestnuts and pineapple in large bowl. Combine mayonnaise, curry, sugar, salt, cayenne and ginger; stir into chicken mixture. Cover and refrigerate until chilled, at least 2 hours. Serve on lettuce leaves. Sprinkle with crumbled bacon.

Yields 6 servings

Paella Salad

1	6-OUNCE PACKAGE FROZEN, PEELED, DEVEINED, COOKED SHRIMP
3	CUPS COOKED YELLOW OR WHITE RICE, COOLED
1	8-OUNCE CAN MINCED CLAMS, DRAINED
1 1/2	CUPS DICED COOKED CHICKEN
1 1/2	CUPS SLICED CELERY
1 1/2	CUPS COOKED PEAS
1/2	CUP DICED RED OR GREEN PEPPER
1/3	CUP SLICED GREEN ONIONS
1/3	CUP SLICED RIPE OLIVES
	SALT AND PEPPER TO TASTE
	ITALIAN SALAD DRESSING

Combine shrimp, rice, clams, chicken, celery, peas, red bell pepper, green onions and olives in large bowl. Season with salt and pepper to taste. Garnish with tomato slices and serve with Italian or your favorite salad dressing.

Yields 6 to 8 servings

Marinated Catfish Salad

2	CATFISH FILLETS, CUT INTO 1-INCH PIECES
1	MEDIUM RED BELL AND YELLOW PEPPER, ROASTED AND CUT INTO STRIPS
1	SMALL RED ONION, SLICED AND SEPARATED INTO RINGS
1	TEASPOON DRIED DILL WEED
1/4	CUP OIL
1/4	CUP BALSAMIC VINEGAR
1	CLOVE GARLIC, CRUSHED
6	CUPS ASSORTED SALAD GREENS
4	STRIPS BACON, COOKED CRISP AND CRUMBLED
	SALT AND PEPPER TO TASTE

Place catfish pieces in skillet; add enough water to cover. Cook over low heat for 5 to 7 minutes or until fish flakes easily with fork. Drain. Combine catfish pieces, pepper strips, onion rings, dill weed, oil, vinegar and garlic in large bowl. Cover; marinate for 1 hour. Just before serving toss with lettuce, bacon, salt and pepper to taste. Garnish with parsley if desired.

Yields 4 servings

Caribbean Lobster Salad

2 TABLESPOONS FRESH LEMON OR LIME JUICE

1/2 CUP MAYONNAISE

12 OUNCES COOKED LOBSTER, CUT IN 1/2-INCH PIECES

1/4 CUP DICED CUCUMBER

1/4 CUP CHOPPED ONION

1/4 CUP CHOPPED CELERY

1/4 CUP CHOPPED GREEN OR RED BELL PEPPER

SALT AND PEPPER TO TASTE

DASH HOT PEPPER SAUCE

Combine the juice and mayonnaise. Gently toss with remaining ingredients. Chill. Serve on salad greens.

NOTE: Shrimp or crab meat may be substituted for lobster.

Yields 6 servings

Fresh Corn Salad

5 MEDIUM EARS CORN

1 1/2 CUPS CHOPPED CELERY

1/2 CUP CHOPPED GREEN PEPPER

3 HARD-BOILED EGG WHITES, CHOPPED

2 TABLESPOONS DICED PIMIENTO

1/2 CUP REDUCED-CALORIE MAYONNAISE OR SALAD DRESSING

1 TEASPOON GRATED ONION

2 TEASPOONS FRESH LEMON JUICE

1 TEASPOON SUGAR

1 TEASPOON SALT, OPTIONAL

1/4 TEASPOON PEPPER

DASH HOT PEPPER SAUCE

Cook corn; cool and cut from cob. Mix with celery, green pepper, eggs and pimiento. Combine remaining ingredients; stir into corn mixture. Cover and chill 2 to 4 hours. Nice for stuffed tomatoes if desired.

Yields 6 servings

Fruit Salad With Honey Sesame Salad Dressing

FRUIT SALAD

2 CUPS STRAWBERRY HALVES

1 SMALL PINEAPPLE, PARED AND CUBED

2 KIWIFRUIT, PEELED AND SLICED

HONEY SESAME DRESSING

2 TABLESPOONS VEGETABLE OIL

1 TABLESPOON FRESH LEMON OR LIME JUICE

1 TO 2 TABLESPOONS HONEY

1 TEASPOON SESAME SEEDS

Mix strawberries, pineapple and kiwi in large bowl. Shake vegetable oil, lemon juice, honey and sesame seeds in tightly covered container. Pour over fruit mixture and toss gently to coat fruit. Serve on salad greens and sprinkle with additional sesame seeds if desired.

Yields 4 servings

Spinach-Mushroom Salad

1/3 CUP VEGETABLE OIL
1/4 CUP WINE VINEGAR
1/4 TEASPOON SALT
DASH PEPPER
1 CLOVE GARLIC, CRUSHED
1 POUND SPINACH, TORN INTO BITE-SIZE PIECES, (ABOUT 8 CUPS)
2 OUNCES FRESH MUSHROOMS, SLICED
2 SLICES BACON, CRISPLY COOKED AND CRUMBLED
1 HARD-COOKED EGG, CHOPPED

Shake oil, vinegar, salt, pepper and garlic in tightly covered container. Toss with spinach and mushrooms; sprinkle with crumbled bacon and chopped eggs.

Yields 6 servings

Black-Eyed Peas And Shrimp Salad

1 16-OUNCE PACKAGE BLACK-EYED PEAS
1/4 POUND COOKED SMALL SHRIMP, PEELED AND DEVEINED
1/2 CUP SLICED CELERY
1/2 CUP DICED RED BELL PEPPER
6 GREEN ONIONS, SLICED
1/4 CUP VEGETABLE OIL
2 TABLESPOONS BALSAMIC VINEGAR
1 CLOVE GARLIC, MINCED
SALT AND PEPPER TO TASTE
1 SMALL BIBB LETTUCE, SEPARATED INTO LEAVES

Cook peas as directed on package; drain and cool. Gently toss peas, shrimp, celery, red bell pepper and green onions together in medium bowl. Combine oil, vinegar, garlic, salt and pepper. Pour over shrimp mixture and toss to coat. Chill. Serve on lettuce leaves. Garnish with lemon and parsley if desired.

Yields 4 servings

Mixed Cabbage Cole Slaw

1 MEDIUM GREEN CABBAGE, FINELY SHREDDED
1/2 MEDIUM RED CABBAGE, FINELY SHREDDED
4 MEDIUM CARROTS, PEELED AND GRATED
6 GREEN ONIONS, THINLY SLICED
1/4 CUP CHOPPED GREEN PEPPER
1/4 CUP CHOPPED PIMIENTOS
1 CUP PREPARED COLE SLAW DRESSING
DASH HOT PEPPER SAUCE

Combine green cabbage, red cabbage, carrots, onions, green pepper and pimientos in large bowl. Add dash hot pepper sauce to dressing. Pour dressing mixture over vegetables and toss thoroughly to coat.

Yields 6 to 8 servings

Classic French Salad Dressing

1/2	CUP VEGETABLE OIL
2	TABLESPOONS WINE VINEGAR
2	TABLESPOONS FRESH LEMON JUICE
1/2	TEASPOON SALT
1/2	TEASPOON SUGAR
1/4	TEASPOON DRY MUSTARD
1/4	TEASPOON PAPRIKA

Shake all ingredients well in tightly covered jar. Refrigerate. Shake again just before serving.

Yields about 3/4 cup

Lite Vinaigrette

2	TABLESPOONS OLIVE OIL OR VEGETABLE OIL
2	TABLESPOONS RED WINE VINEGAR
2	TABLESPOONS CARBONATED WATER
2	TABLESPOONS FRESH LEMON JUICE
1	TABLESPOON DIJON-STYLE MUSTARD
2	TABLESPOONS THINLY SLICED GREEN ONION
	SALT AND PEPPER TO TASTE

Combine all ingredients in tightly covered container; refrigerate overnight.

Yields 3/4 cup (1 tablespoon about 25 calories)

Herbed Buttermilk Dressing

1	CUP BUTTERMILK
1	CUP MAYONNAISE
1 1/2	TEASPOONS FINELY CHOPPED PARSLEY
1/2	TEASPOON SALT, OPTIONAL
1/2	TEASPOON DRIED CHIVES
1/4	TEASPOON DRIED OREGANO
1/4	TEASPOON DRIED BASIL
1/4	TEASPOON DRIED TARRAGON
1	CLOVE GARLIC, FINELY MINCED
1/4	TEASPOON PEPPER
1 1/2	TEASPOONS FRESH LEMON JUICE

Shake all ingredients in tightly covered container. Store in refrigerator.

Yields 2 cups

POULTRY

Lemon-Herbed Cornish Hens

Spicy Cornish Hens and Vegetables

2	TABLESPOONS OLIVE OIL
3	CORNISH HENS, CUT INTO QUARTERS
1	TEASPOON CAYENNE PEPPER
	SEASONING SALT TO TASTE
4	MEDIUM RED POTATOES, UNPEELED, AND THICKLY SLICED
6	SMALL ONIONS, PEELED
3	MEDIUM CARROTS, CUT INTO 1-INCH PIECES
2	CELERY RIBS, CUT INTO 1-INCH, DIAGONALLY SLICED PIECES
2	LARGE CLOVES GARLIC, MINCED
1	TEASPOON DRIED THYME
1/4	TEASPOON DRIED ROSEMARY
1	CUP CHICKEN BROTH
	CHOPPED PARSLEY

Heat oven to 350 degrees. Heat oil in large oven-proof skillet or Dutch oven over medium-high heat. Sprinkle cornish hens with cayenne pepper and seasoning salt. Add the cornish hens in single layer (you may need to do this in batches) and brown on both sides. Remove from the skillet; set aside. Add potato slices and brown on both sides, about 3 minutes. Return the hens to pan. Add onions, carrots, celery and garlic. Sprinkle with thyme and rosemary. Pour broth over and cover tightly. Bake in oven until hens are done and vegetables are tender, about 30 minutes. Place hens on heated serving platter and spoon the vegetables around them. Heat remaining liquid in skillet until desired consistency. Spoon sauce over hens and vegetables. Garnish with chopped parsley.

Yields 6 servings

Oven-Fried Chicken

1	2 1/2- TO 3-POUND BROILER-FRYER
1/2	TEASPOON SALT
1/4	TEASPOON PEPPER
1/2	TEASPOON GARLIC POWDER
1/2	CUP ALL-PURPOSE FLOUR
1	TEASPOON PAPRIKA
	VEGETABLE COOKING SPRAY
2	TABLESPOONS REDUCED-CALORIE MARGARINE, MELTED

Trim all visible fat from chicken. Season chicken parts with salt, pepper and garlic powder. Combine flour and paprika in medium bowl. Coat seasoned chicken parts with flour mixture. Spray rectangular 13x9x2-inch pan with vegetable cooking spray. Place chicken pieces skin-side down in pan. Drizzle melted margarine over chicken. Bake uncovered at 425 degrees for 30 minutes. Turn chicken; bake until thickest pieces are done, about 30 minutes longer.

NOTE: Skin may be removed from chicken if desired.

Yields 6 servings

Cajun Fried Chicken

1	CUP ALL-PURPOSE FLOUR
2	TEASPOONS SALT
1	TEASPOON GARLIC POWDER
1 1/2	TEASPOONS PAPRIKA
1	TEASPOON DRIED THYME, CRUSHED
1	TEASPOON DRIED OREGANO, CRUSHED
1/2	TEASPOON BLACK PEPPER
1/4	TEASPOON WHITE PEPPER
1/2 TO 1	TEASPOON CAYENNE PEPPER
1	2 1/2- TO 3-POUND BROILER-FRYER CHICKEN, CUT UP
2	EGGS BEATEN

Mix together 1/2 cup flour, salt, garlic powder, paprika, thyme, oregano, black pepper, white pepper and cayenne pepper in bowl; set aside. Coat chicken pieces with remaining 1/2 cup flour; shake off excess flour. Dip chicken pieces in beaten eggs, then coat chicken with seasoned flour mixture.

Heat oil (about 1/2 inch) in 12-inch skillet over medium-high heat until hot. Add chicken, skin-side down, and brown quickly on all sides, about 10 minutes. Reduce heat to low; cover and cook until thickest pieces are done, about 30 minutes, turning once or twice. Remove cover during last 5 minutes of cooking to crispen chicken.

Yields 6 servings

Champagne-Mushroom Chicken

2	TABLESPOONS ALL-PURPOSE FLOUR
1/2	TEASPOON SALT, OPTIONAL
1/2	TEASPOON GARLIC POWDER
1/4	TEASPOON PAPRIKA
1/4	TEASPOON WHITE PEPPER
4	CHICKEN BREAST HALVES, SKINNED AND BONED
1	TABLESPOON REDUCED-CALORIE MARGARINE
1	TABLESPOON VEGETABLE OIL
3/4	CUP CHAMPAGNE, OR DRY WHITE WINE
1	CUP THINLY SLICED FRESH MUSHROOMS
1/2	CUP EVAPORATED SKIMMED MILK
2	TABLESPOONS CHOPPED PARSLEY

Combine flour, salt, garlic powder, paprika and pepper. Lightly coat chicken in flour mixture. Heat margarine and oil in 10-inch skillet over medium heat. Add chicken and brown 4 minutes on each side. Add champagne and continue to cook over medium heat until chicken is done, about 10 min-

utes. Remove chicken to platter and keep warm. Add mushrooms and milk to skillet. Cook over low heat, stirring constantly, until thickened. Return chicken to sauce, spooning sauce over until chicken is warmed through. Garnish with parsley if desired.

Yields 4 servings

Chicken Wrap Sandwich
With Lemon Mayonnaise

4	WHOLE WHEAT OR FLOUR TORTILLAS
4	BONELESS SKINLESS CHICKEN BREAST HALVES, COOKED AS DESIRED AND CUT INTO STRIPS
1	SMALL RED OR GREEN BELL PEPPER, CUT INTO STRIPS
1/2	SMALL SWEET ONION, THINLY SLICED
2	PLUM TOMATOES, DICED
1	CUP ROMAINE LETTUCE, TORN INTO BITE-SIZE PIECES
1/2	TEASPOON DRIED BASIL
	SALT AND PEPPER TO TASTE
1/2	CUP MAYONNAISE
1	TABLESPOON FRESH LEMON JUICE
1	CLOVE GARLIC, FINELY MINCED

Combine chicken, red bell pepper, onion, tomatoes, lettuce, basil, salt and pepper in medium bowl. Mix together mayonnaise, lemon juice and garlic until well-blended in small bowl. Divide chicken mixture among tortillas; spoon filling into bottom quarter. Fold bottom flap over filling, then fold the two sides in toward center, overlapping slightly to close. Serve with lemon mayonnaise.

Yields 4 servings

Jerk Chicken

1 1/2 TEASPOONS GROUND ALLSPICE

1 TEASPOON DRIED THYME

1/2 TO 1 TEASPOON CAYENNE PEPPER

1/2 TEASPOON BLACK PEPPER

1/2 TEASPOON GROUND NUTMEG

1/2 TEASPOON GROUND CINNAMON

1 TEASPOON SALT

1 TEASPOON GARLIC POWDER

2 TEASPOONS SUGAR

2 TABLESPOONS VEGETABLE OIL

JUICE OF 1 LIME

1/4 CUP ORANGE JUICE

1 SMALL ONION, FINELY CHOPPED

1 SCOTCH BONNET PEPPER, SEEDED AND FINELY CHOPPED

1/4 CUP FINELY CHOPPED GREEN ONION

1 2 1/2- TO 3-POUND BROILER-FRYER CHICKEN, CUT IN SERVING-SIZE PIECES

Place all ingredients except chicken in blender or food processor. Using pulse speed, blend until ingredients are well-blended. Place chicken parts in glass or plastic bowl. Pour marinade over chicken and toss to coat. Cover and refrigerate for 4 or more hours.

Heat grill until coals turn white. Place chicken pieces skin-side down on grill. Turn chicken every 10 minutes, basting occasionally with marinade. Slowly cook chicken until done, about 1½ hours. Heat remaining marinade to boiling and serve with chicken if desired.

Yields 4 servings

Rosemary-Orange Chicken Breast

6 BONELESS CHICKEN BREAST HALVES

1/2 TO 3/4 TEASPOON DRIED ROSEMARY, CRUSHED

1/4 TEASPOON PEPPER

1 TABLESPOON VEGETABLE OIL

2 CUPS FRESH ORANGE JUICE

1 TEASPOON GRATED ORANGE RIND

PARSLEY

Remove skin from chicken; sprinkle chicken with rosemary and pepper. Heat oil in 10-inch skillet. Brown chicken in oil over medium heat until light brown on both sides. Pour off fat. Stir in orange juice and orange rind; reduce heat. Cover and cook 20 minutes, stirring occasionally. Remove cover and continue to cook until sauce has thickened. Garnish with parsley if desired.

Yields 6 servings

Chicken in Groundnut Sauce

2 TABLESPOONS PEANUT OR VEGETABLE OIL

1 2 1/2- TO 3-POUND BROILER-FRYER CHICKEN, CUT UP

1/4 CUP DRIED SHRIMP

1 CUP HOT WATER

2 TABLESPOONS TOMATO PASTE

1 14 ½-OUNCE CAN WHOLE TOMATOES, UNDRAINED

1 MEDIUM ONION, CHOPPED

3 CLOVES GARLIC, FINELY CHOPPED

1 TEASPOON CRUSHED RED PEPPER

1/4 TEASPOON GROUND GINGER

2 TEASPOONS CHILI POWDER

1/2   TEASPOON SALT, OPTIONAL

1/2 TO 1 CUP CRUNCHY PEANUT BUTTER

Heat oil in Dutch oven until hot. Cook chicken over medium heat until brown on all sides, about 15 minutes. Remove chicken. Drain fat from Dutch oven. Heat dried shrimp, water, tomato paste, tomatoes, onion, garlic, crushed red pepper, ginger, chili powder and salt to boiling in Dutch oven; reduce heat. Cover and simmer 10 minutes. Add chicken; cover and simmer 45 minutes.

Stir some of the hot liquid into peanut butter; stir into chicken mixture. Turn chicken to coat with sauce. Cover and cook until chicken is done, 10 to 15 minutes. Serve with chopped peanuts.

Yields 6 servings

Chicken, Tomato And Rice

　　VEGETABLE COOKING SPRAY

1　　2 1/2- TO 3-POUND BROILER-FRYER, CUT UP

1　　10½-OUNCE CAN CONDENSED CHICKEN BROTH

1　　14½-OUNCE CAN TOMATOES, UNDRAINED AND CUT UP

1/3　CUP WATER

1/2　CUP CHOPPED ONION

1/2　CUP CHOPPED GREEN PEPPER

2　　LARGE CLOVES GARLIC, MINCED

1/2　TEASPOON SALT, OPTIONAL

1/4　TEASPOON TURMERIC OR SAFFRON, OPTIONAL

1/8 TO 1/4 TEASPOON CRUSHED RED PEPPER

1　　BAY LEAF

1　　CUP CONVERTED BRAND RICE

　　SLICED OLIVES

Spray Dutch oven or large skillet with veg-etable cooking spray. Brown chicken parts on both sides over medium heat until golden brown, about 15 minutes; pour off fat. Add broth, tomatoes, water, onion, green pepper, garlic, salt, turmeric, red pepper and bay leaf. Cover and bring to a boil; reduce heat to low and cook for 30 minutes. Add rice; cover and cook 30 minutes more or until rice is done and most of the water is absorbed. Garnish with sliced green or ripe olives if desired.

Yields 6 servings

Lemon-Herbed Cornish Hens

6　　CORNISH HENS (ABOUT 1 1/2 POUNDS EACH)

1/4　CUP REDUCED-CALORIE MARGARINE, MELTED

2　　TABLESPOONS FRESH LEMON JUICE

2　　TEASPOONS FINELY CHOPPED PARSLEY

1/2　TEASPOON DRIED THYME, CRUSHED

1/4　TEASPOON DRIED ROSEMARY, CRUSHED

1　　CLOVE GARLIC, CRUSHED

Remove giblets and necks from hens; rinse and drain hens. (Use giblets and necks for broth if desired.) Tuck neck skin under wings to secure it. Place hens breast-side up on rack in roasting pan. Combine remaining ingredients; brush hens with mixture. Roast uncovered in 350-degree oven until hens are done, brushing occasionally with margarine mixture, about 1½ hours.

Yields 6 servings

Skillet Chicken and Dumplings

1/2   CUP ALL-PURPOSE FLOUR
1   TEASPOON PAPRIKA
    SALT AND PEPPER TO TASTE
1   2 1/2- TO 3-POUND BROILER-FRYER CHICKEN, CUT UP
    VEGETABLE OIL
1   CUP CHICKEN BROTH
1/2   TEASPOON DRIED THYME, CRUSHED
1/4   TEASPOON GARLIC POWDER
3   TABLESPOONS ALL-PURPOSE FLOUR
    MILK
    DUMPLINGS

Combine 1/2 cup flour, paprika, salt and pepper. Coat chicken parts with flour mixture. Heat thin layer of oil in large skillet; brown chicken on all sides. Drain off drippings; reserve for later. Add broth, thyme and garlic powder to skillet. Cover and cook chicken 35 minutes or until fork tender, adding water if necessary. Remove chicken and keep warm. Pour off liquid in skillet; reserve for later.

To make gravy, heat 3 tablespoons reserved drippings in skillet. Blend in 3 tablespoons flour. Cook over low heat, stirring until mixture is smooth and bubbly. Remove from heat. Add enough milk to reserved broth to measure 3 cups; pour into skillet. Heat to boiling, stirring constantly. Boil and stir 1 minute. Return chicken to gravy. Prepare dough for Dumplings; drop by spoonfuls onto hot chicken. Cook uncovered for 10 minutes; cover and cook 20 minutes longer.

Yields 6 to 8 servings

DUMPLINGS

1 1/2   CUPS ALL-PURPOSE FLOUR
2   TEASPOONS BAKING POWDER
1/2   TEASPOON SALT
3   TABLESPOONS SHORTENING
3   TABLESPOONS CHOPPED PARSLEY
3/4   CUP MILK

Combine flour, baking powder and salt into bowl. Cut in shortening until mixture looks like meal. Stir in parsley. Stir in milk.

Chicken and Sausage Jambalaya

4   TABLESPOONS VEGETABLE OIL
1   POUND ANDOUILLE OR HOT SMOKED SAUSAGE, CUT INTO 1/2-INCH SLICES
1   CUP CHOPPED CELERY
1   LARGE ONION, CHOPPED
2   GREEN OR RED BELL PEPPERS, CHOPPED
3   GARLIC CLOVES, MINCED
3   CUPS CHICKEN BROTH
1   15-OUNCE CAN WHOLE PEELED TOMATOES, COARSELY CHOPPED, UNDRAINED
2   BAY LEAVES
1   TEASPOON PEPPER SAUCE
1/2   TEASPOON DRIED OREGANO
1/2   TEASPOON DRIED THYME
1/4   TEASPOON GROUND ALLSPICE
1 1/2   CUPS RAW RICE
1   POUND COOKED CHICKEN, CUT IN 1-INCH PIECES

Heat oil over medium-high heat in large heavy saucepan or Dutch oven. Add sausage, celery, onion, bell pepper and garlic. Cook for 5 minutes or until vegetables are tender; stir frequently. Stir in broth, tomatoes, bay leaves, pepper sauce, oregano, thyme and allspice. Bring to a boil. Reduce heat and simmer uncovered for 10 minutes; stir occasionally. Stir in rice. Cover, simmer 15 minutes. Add chicken; cover and simmer 5 minutes longer or until rice is tender. Let stand covered 10 minutes. Remove bay leaves. Garnish with parsley if desired.

Yields 8 servings

Curried Chicken

1	2 1/2- TO 3-POUND BROILER-FRYER CHICKEN
1	MEDIUM ONION, CHOPPED
1	MEDIUM TOMATO, PEELED AND CHOPPED (OPTIONAL)
2	TEASPOONS FRESH LEMON JUICE
2	CLOVES GARLIC, MINCED
1/2	TEASPOON DRIED THYME, CRUSHED
3	TABLESPOONS CURRY POWDER
	SALT AND PEPPER TO TASTE
1	TEASPOON VEGETABLE OIL
1	TEASPOON CUMIN SEED

Cut the meat off the chicken bones into bite-size pieces. Combine onion, tomato, lemon juice, 1 clove garlic, thyme, 2 tablespoons curry powder, salt and pepper. Place chicken pieces in shallow glass dish; pour seasoning over chicken, stirring to make sure chicken is coated with marinade. Refrigerate in marinade for 2 or 3 hours. Heat oil in heavy 10-inch skillet. Add cumin seed and the remaining garlic. Cook until dark brown. Stir in remaining curry powder. Add marinaded chicken mixture. Cook until chicken is well-browned; reduce heat and cover. Continue to cook until chicken is done, about 15 to 20 minutes. Serve with rice.

Yields 6 servings

Chicken Patties

4	CUPS FINELY CHOPPED COOKED CHICKEN OR TURKEY
1/2	CUP FINELY CHOPPED CELERY
1/2	CUP FINELY CHOPPED ONION
2	TABLESPOONS FINELY CHOPPED RED BELL PEPPER
1/2	TEASPOON POULTRY SEASONING
	SALT AND PEPPER TO TASTE
2	EGGS, SLIGHTLY BEATEN
	DRY BREAD CRUMBS
1/4	CUP VEGETABLE OIL

Mix together chicken, celery, onion, red bell pepper, poultry seasoning, salt and pepper in medium bowl. Pour beaten eggs over chicken mixture and mix well; chill. Shape into 8 to 10 patties. Coat each patty with bread crumbs. Heat oil in 10-inch skillet over medium heat until hot. Cook patties on each side until golden brown, about 10 minutes. Serve immediately. Serve with Sweet and Sour Sauce if desired.

Yields 8 to 10 servings

Herb-Roasted Capon

1 6- TO 8-POUND CAPON
1 TEASPOON SEASONING SALT
1 TEASPOON THYME, CRUSHED
1/4 TEASPOON ROSEMARY, CRUSHED
1/4 TEASPOON RUBBED SAGE
1/4 TEASPOON BLACK PEPPER
1/8 TEASPOON GARLIC POWDER
 VEGETABLE OIL

Remove giblets and neck from inside bird. Rinse bird with running cold water and drain well. Combine seasoning salt, thyme, rosemary, sage, pepper and garlic powder and rub over outside and inside body cavity. Cover and refrigerate at least 12 hours or overnight. Brush skin with oil; roast uncovered in 325-degree oven for 3 to 4 hours or until done, basting frequently.

Yields 8 servings

Chicken Fajitas

4 CHICKEN BREAST HALVES, BONED AND SKINNED
 JUICE FROM 1 LIME
1/4 CUP PINEAPPLE JUICE
1 CLOVE GARLIC, MINCED
2 TABLESPOONS VEGETABLE OIL
 SALT, PEPPER AND CHILI POWDER TO TASTE
 FLOUR TORTILLAS
 GUACAMOLE
 SALSA

Place chicken breast in glass dish. Combine juices, oil and garlic. Pour over chicken; turn to coat all sides. Marinate 30 minutes or more. Remove chicken from marinade; season with salt, pepper and chili powder.

Place chicken on greased broiler rack in foil-lined broiler pan so that top of chicken is 5 to 7 inches from heat. Brush on marinade every 10 to 15 minutes and turn chicken as it browns. Broil until done, 20 minutes. Remove from broiler and slice into thin strips. Serve chicken piled on hot flour tortillas and top with guacamole and salsa.

Yields 4 servings

Chicken Spinach-Caesar Wrap

1 CUP SHREDDED JARLSBERG LITE CHEESE
2 CUPS COOKED, SHREDDED CHICKEN
3/4 CUP NON-FAT CAESAR SALAD DRESSING
4 CUPS SPINACH LEAVES, WASHED AND DRIED (ABOUT 4 OUNCES)
4 10-INCH FLOUR TORTILLAS

Mix Jarlsberg cheese and chicken in bowl and toss well with dressing; set aside.

Arrange 1 cup spinach leaves on one side of a tortilla. Spoon on 1/4 chicken mixture. Roll up tightly, tucking in ends. Repeat to make 4.

Wrap in microwave-safe paper and refrigerate. Heat in microwave 1½ to 2 minutes or until warm. Slice in half.

Yields 4 wraps

Turkey Burgers

1   POUND GROUND TURKEY
1/4   CUP DRY BREAD CRUMBS
1/4   CUP FINELY CHOPPED ONION
1   EGG OR 2 EGG WHITES
1/2   TEASPOON GARLIC POWDER
1/4   TEASPOON PEPPER
      VEGETABLE COOKING SPRAY
      LETTUCE, TOMATO AND ONION SLICES

Combine all ingredients except vegetable cooking spray in medium bowl. Shape turkey mixture into 4 patties, each about 1/2 inch thick.

Spray large skillet with vegetable cooking spray. Heat skillet until hot over medium heat. Place patties in pan and cook for 5 minutes on each side until brown. Cover and cook over low heat for 10 minutes longer or until cooked through. Serve on toasted hamburger buns with lettuce, tomatoes and onion slices if desired.

Yields 4 servings

Turkey Chili

1   POUND GROUND TURKEY
1   MEDIUM ONION, CHOPPED
1   SMALL GREEN PEPPER, CHOPPED
3   LARGE CLOVES GARLIC, MINCED
3   TABLESPOONS CHILI POWDER
1   TEASPOON DRIED OREGANO, CRUSHED
1/2   TEASPOON GROUND CUMIN
1/4 TO 1/2 TEASPOON CRUSHED RED PEPPER
1   14½-OUNCE CAN TOMATOES, UNDRAINED AND CUT UP
1   15-OUNCE CAN CHILI BEANS, UNDRAINED
1   16-OUNCE CAN TOMATO SAUCE

1   TEASPOON SUGAR

Cook and stir ground turkey with onion, green pepper, garlic, chili powder, oregano, cumin and crushed red pepper over medium heat until turkey is brown, about 10 minutes. Stir in tomatoes, chili beans, tomato sauce and sugar. Bring turkey mixture to a boil; reduce heat and simmer uncovered for 30 to 45 minutes or until desired consistency, stirring occasionally.

Yields 6 servings

Chicken Wrap Sandwich with Lemon Mayonnaise

Smothered Chicken With Herbs

1/4   TEASPOON DRIED THYME, CRUSHED
1/4   TEASPOON POULTRY SEASONING
     SALT AND PEPPER TO TASTE
1   2 1/2- TO 3-POUND BROILER-FRYER CHICKEN, CUT UP
1/3   CUP ALL-PURPOSE FLOUR
1/4   CUP VEGETABLE OIL
1 1/2   CUPS WATER
1   SMALL ONION, THINLY SLICED

Combine thyme, poultry seasoning, salt and pepper. Season chicken with herb mixture. Coat chicken with flour. Heat oil in large skillet. Brown chicken on all sides over medium heat; remove from skillet. Slowly brown remaining flour mixture in oil until golden brown, stirring constantly. Slowly stir in water. Add additional salt to gravy if desired. Return chicken to skillet; add onion. Cover and cook over low heat until done , about 25 to 30 minutes.

Yields 4 to 6 servings

Orange-Herbed Chicken And Rice

3 TO 3 1/2 POUNDS CHICKEN PARTS
1 1/2 CUPS ORANGE JUICE
1/4   CUP DRY WHITE WINE
2   TEASPOONS DRIED OREGANO, CRUSHED
1/2   TEASPOON GARLIC POWDER
1/2   TEASPOON GROUND SAGE
1/2   TEASPOON DRIED ROSEMARY, CRUSHED
1/2   TEASPOON DRIED THYME, CRUSHED
     SALT AND PEPPER TO TASTE
     PAPRIKA

1/4   CUP ORANGE MARMALADE
1   TABLESPOON CORNSTARCH
3   CUPS HOT COOKED RICE

Place chicken in 13x9-inch baking dish, skin-side down. Combine juice, wine and seasonings. Pour over chicken. Sprinkle with paprika. Cover and bake at 350 degrees for 30 minutes. Turn chicken; sprinkle with paprika. Bake uncovered for 30 minutes longer or until chicken is done. Pour pan juices into saucepan; skim fat. Add marmalade and cornstarch dissolved in 2 tablespoons water. Cook, stirring until sauce is clear and thickened. Serve chicken and sauce over bed of rice. Garnish with orange slices.

Yields 6 servings

Spicy Oven-Barbecued Chicken

1   2 1/2- TO 3-POUND BROILER-FRYER CHICKEN, CUT UP
     SALT AND PEPPER TO TASTE
1   CUP BOTTLED BARBECUE SAUCE
2   TABLESPOONS HONEY
1   TABLESPOON CHILI POWDER
1   CLOVE GARLIC, MINCED
1/2   TEASPOON RED PEPPER SAUCE
1/4   TEASPOON DRIED OREGANO

Season chicken with salt and pepper. Place chicken, skin-side up, in ungreased 13x9x2-inch rectangular pan. Mix remaining ingredients together in small bowl. Bake chicken at 375 degrees for 40 minutes. Pour sauce over chicken; bake uncovered until thickest pieces are done, about 20 to 30 minutes.

Yields 6 servings

MEATS

Bourbon-Barbecued Ribs

Bourbon-Barbecued Ribs

1   CUP KETCHUP
1/3   CUP BOURBON
1/4   CUP MOLASSES
2   TABLESPOONS VINEGAR
1   TABLESPOON WORCESTERSHIRE SAUCE
1   TABLESPOON SOY SAUCE
1/2   TEASPOON DRY MUSTARD
2   CLOVES GARLIC, FINELY MINCED
1   TABLESPOON LEMON JUICE
    HOT PEPPER SAUCE TO TASTE
4 1/2   POUNDS FRESH PORK SPARERIBS, CUT INTO SERVING-SIZE PIECES

Mix all ingredients except spareribs; let stand at room temperature for 1½ hours. Place pork spareribs, meaty-side up, on rack in shallow roasting pan. Roast uncovered in 325-degree oven for 1½ hours. Brush sauce over ribs. Roast, turning and brushing frequently with sauce, until ribs are done, about 30 minutes longer. Heat remaining sauce to boiling, stirring occasionally. Serve with ribs.

NOTE: This sauce also can be used on chicken or hamburgers.

Yields 4 servings

Braised Short Ribs

    VEGETABLE COOKING SPRAY
3   POUNDS BEEF SHORT RIBS
1/2   CUP TOMATO JUICE
1/4   CUP WATER
6   CARROTS, CUT INTO 2-INCH PIECES
6   MEDIUM POTATOES
6   SMALL ONIONS
3   STALKS CELERY, CUT INTO 2-INCH PIECES
1/2   TEASPOON GARLIC POWDER
    SALT AND PEPPER TO TASTE

Coat large skillet with vegetable cooking spray. Heat skillet over medium heat. Add short ribs and brown on all sides. Reduce heat to medium-low. Add tomato juice and water; cover and simmer 1½ hours. Skim off fat. Add carrots, potatoes, onions, celery, garlic powder, salt and pepper. Cover and continue to cook until meat and vegetables are tender, about 1 hour. Additional tomato juice may be added if needed. Garnish with parsley if desired.

Yields 6 to 8 servings

Standing Rib Roast

1   6- TO 8-POUND STANDING RIB ROAST
2   LARGE CLOVES GARLIC, CRUSHED
1/2   TEASPOON DRIED ROSEMARY
1/2   TEASPOON SEASONING SALT
1/4   TEASPOON PEPPER
1   ONION, THICKLY SLICED
1   CUP DRY RED WINE
2   CUPS BEEF BROTH

Heat oven to 325 degrees. Trim most of the visible fat from meat. Place roast bone-side down in shallow roasting pan. Rub garlic over meat. Sprinkle rosemary over meat. Season with seasoning salt and pepper. Arrange onion around roast. Pour 1/2 cup of the wine over meat. Roast meat with meat thermometer inserted in center until desired doneness, basting frequently with pan juices, about every 30 minutes.

Transfer meat to heated platter, reserving dripping in pan. Place foil over meat to keep warm. Skim fat off pan drippings. Set pan with drippings over medium-high heat. Add beef broth and remaining wine and boil until syrupy, scraping up any browned bits and stirring frequently, about 8 minutes. Season sauce with additional seasoning salt if needed. Strain sauce. Serve meat with sauce.

TIP: Always allow roasts or other large cuts of meat to rest for 10 to 15 minutes after cooking; it makes slicing the meat easier and allows the juices to set.

Yields 6 to 8 servings

Broiled Flank Steak

1	FLANK STEAK (1 1/2 TO 2 POUNDS)
2	SMALL ONIONS, THINLY SLICED
1	TABLESPOON ORANGE JUICE
1	TABLESPOON SUGAR
1/2	TEASPOON SALT, OPTIONAL
1/2	TEASPOON DRIED OREGANO, CRUSHED
1/8	TEASPOON PEPPER
2	TABLESPOONS SOY SAUCE
1	TABLESPOON VEGETABLE OIL

Score steak 1/8-inch deep on both sides in diamond design. Layer half the onion in large shallow glass dish; place steak over onion and top with remaining onions. Thoroughly combine remaining ingredients; pour over steak and onions. Cover and refrigerate overnight, turning several times. Preheat oven to 550 degrees or broil. Remove steak from marinade; blot with paper towels. Broil meat 3 to 5 inches from heat; cook 5 minutes on each side, or to desired doneness. While broiling meat, cook onions in skillet until tender. To serve, hold knife almost horizontal to meat and cut into thin diagonal slices; serve with cooked onions.

Yields 4 servings

Peach-Glazed Stuffed Pork Chops

1	8 1/2-OUNCE CAN SLICED PEACHES
1	6-OUNCE PACKAGE CORNBREAD STUFFING MIX
1	CUP HOT WATER
1/4	CUP BUTTER OR MARGARINE
6	PORK CHOPS WITH POCKET (CUT FOR STUFFING 1-INCH THICK)
1/2	CUP PEACH PRESERVES
1	TABLESPOON DIJON MUSTARD

Heat oven to 350 degrees. Drain and dice peaches, reserving syrup. Mix contents of vegetables/seasoning packet, water and butter in bowl; stir in crumbs, peaches and reserved syrup. Fill pork chop pockets with stuffing. Arrange chops in 13x9-inch baking pan. Mix preserves and mustard; brush over chops on both sides. Bake 60 minutes or until cooked through, brushing occasionally with preserve mixture. Bake any remaining stuffing in a casserole for 30 minutes.

Yields 6 servings

Beef Pot Roast

1   TABLESPOON OLIVE OIL

3 1/2 TO 4 POUNDS BEEF CHUCK OR CROSS RIB ROAST

1   MEDIUM ONION, SLICED

1/4 CUP CHOPPED GREEN PEPPER

1/4 CUP CHOPPED RED BELL PEPPER

2   CLOVES GARLIC, MINCED

1/4 TEASPOON DRIED ROSEMARY, CRUSHED

1   8-OUNCE CAN TOMATO SAUCE

1   CUP BEEF BROTH

      SALT AND PEPPER TO TASTE

6   SMALL POTATOES, HALVED

6   CARROTS, QUARTERED

      CHOPPED PARSLEY

Heat oil in Dutch oven over medium heat. Add beef; brown on all sides. Remove roast and place on plate. Cook onion, green pepper, red pepper, garlic and rosemary in Dutch oven until tender. Add tomato sauce and broth; stir to mix. Return beef to pot. Season with salt and pepper. Reduce to low heat; cover and simmer 2 hours. Add potatoes and carrots; cover and continue to cook 30 minutes or until vegetables are tender.

Yields 8 servings

Beef And Peppers Skillet

1 1/2 POUNDS BONELESS BEEF, SIRLOIN TIP, CUT INTO THIN SLICES

1   TABLESPOON CORNSTARCH

2   TABLESPOONS PEANUT OR VEGETABLE OIL

3   TABLESPOONS SOY SAUCE

1   CLOVE GARLIC, MINCED

1   TEASPOON SUGAR

      DASH CAYENNE

1/2 TEASPOON GROUND GINGER

1   MEDIUM GREEN PEPPER, SLICED INTO THIN STRIPS

1   SMALL RED BELL PEPPER, SLICED INTO THIN STRIPS

1/4 POUND FRESH MUSHROOMS, QUARTERED

1   SMALL ONION, SLICED AND SEPARATED INTO RINGS

Combine cornstarch, 1 tablespoon oil, soy sauce, garlic, sugar and cayenne in medium glass bowl. Add beef; toss to coat well. Let stand several hours in refrigerator. Drain and save marinade. Heat ginger in remaining oil in large skillet or wok. Add beef and stir-fry until brown, 5 to 6 minutes. Push to one side. Add green and red bell peppers, mushrooms and onions. Cook until slightly tender, 2 to 3 minutes. Pour reserved marinade over meat and combine with pepper mixture in wok. If necessary, add some water, cook and stir until thickened. Serve with hot rice.

Yields 6 servings

French Pepper Steak

2 TO 4 TEASPOONS WHOLE BLACK PEPPERCORNS

4   BEEF TOP LOIN STRIP STEAKS, CUT 1-INCH THICK

4   TABLESPOONS BUTTER OR MARGARINE

1/4 CUP SLICED GREEN ONIONS

1   TEASPOON INSTANT BEEF BOUILLON

1/3 CUP WATER

1/4 CUP BRANDY

Coarsely crack peppercorns with mortar and pestle or in metal mixing bowl with bottom of a bottle. Place one steak on waxed paper. Sprinkle with 1/4 to 1/2 teaspoon cracked peppercorns; rub over meat and press in with heel of hand. Turn steak and repeat. Continue with remaining steaks. Melt 2 tablespoons butter in large skillet. Cook steak over medium-high heat to desired doneness, 11 to 12 minutes for medium. Season with salt if desired. Transfer to hot serving plate; keep hot.

Cook green onions in remaining 2 tablespoons butter until tender but not brown, about 1 minute. Add bouillon and water; boil rapidly over high heat 1 minute, scraping up browned bits from pan. Add brandy; cook 1 minute more. Pour over steaks.

Yields 4 servings

Rolled Spinach Meat Loaf

1 1/2	POUNDS LEAN GROUND BEEF
1 1/2	CUPS TOMATO SAUCE OR SPAGHETTI SAUCE
1/2	CUP DRY BREAD CRUMBS
1	EGG OR 2 EGG WHITES, SLIGHTLY BEATEN
1/4	CUP FINELY CHOPPED GREEN PEPPER
1/4	CUP FINELY CHOPPED ONION
1	TABLESPOON WORCESTERSHIRE
1	TEASPOON SALT, OPTIONAL
1/2	TEASPOON GARLIC POWDER
1/4	TEASPOON PEPPER
	SHREDDED REDUCED-FAT PART-SKIM MOZZARELLA CHEESE

Combine ground beef, 1/2 cup tomato sauce, bread crumbs, egg, green pepper, onion, Worcestershire sauce, salt, garlic powder and pepper. Mix thoroughly. Pat into a 12x9-inch rectangle on waxed paper. Press spinach filling onto ground beef mixture to within 1 inch of edge. With the aid of waxed paper, roll meat mixture tightly, jelly-roll fashion, starting at long edges. Seal ends; use waxed paper to transfer to shallow baking dish. Bake at 350 degrees for 1 hour. Spoon remaining sauce over meat loaf; sprinkle with shredded Mozzarella cheese. Bake until cheese melts, about 5 minutes.

SPINACH FILLING

1	10-OUNCE PACKAGE FROZEN CHOPPED SPINACH, THAWED AND WELL-DRAINED
3	GREEN ONIONS, THINLY SLICED
1	4-OUNCE CAN MUSHROOM STEMS AND PIECES, DRAINED AND CHOPPED
1/2	CUP SHREDDED REDUCED-FAT PART-SKIM MOZZARELLA CHEESE
	DASH NUTMEG
	SALT AND PEPPER TO TASTE

Combine all ingredients in small bowl.

Yields 6 servings

Corned Beef Hash

2	CUPS CHOPPED COOKED CORNED BEEF
2	CUPS DICED COOKED POTATOES
1	MEDIUM ONION, CHOPPED
1/2	TEASPOON DRIED THYME, CRUSHED
	SALT AND PEPPER TO TASTE
2	TABLESPOONS VEGETABLE OIL
2	TABLESPOONS BUTTER OR MARGARINE
2	TABLESPOONS CHOPPED PARSLEY

Combine corned beef, potatoes, onion, thyme, salt and pepper in large bowl. Heat oil with butter in 10-inch heavy skillet until butter is melted. Spread corned beef mixture evenly in skillet. Fry, turning frequently, until lightly browned, 10 to 15 minutes. Sprinkle with parsley.

Yields 4 servings

Hearty Beer Chili

2 POUNDS SIRLOIN, CUT INTO 1/2-INCH CUBES
1 LARGE ONION, CHOPPED
1 SMALL GREEN PEPPER, CHOPPED
4 CLOVES GARLIC, MINCED
2 TO 3 TABLESPOONS CHILI POWDER
1 1/2 TEASPOONS GROUND CUMIN
1 TEASPOON DRIED OREGANO, CRUSHED
1/4 TEASPOON DRIED CORIANDER, CRUSHED
2 TABLESPOONS OLIVE OIL
1 28-OUNCE CAN PLUM TOMATOES, UNDRAINED AND CUT-UP
1 15-OUNCE CAN TOMATO SAUCE
1 CUP BEEF BROTH
1 CUP FLAT BEER
1 TO 2 TABLESPOONS PACKED BROWN SUGAR
SALT AND PEPPER TO TASTE
DASH CRUSHED RED PEPPER
2 15½-OUNCE CANS CHILI BEANS, UNDRAINED

Cook and stir beef, onion, green pepper, garlic, chili powder, cumin, oregano and coriander in oil in Dutch oven until meat is brown. Add remaining ingredients except beans. Heat to boiling. Reduce heat; cover and simmer for about 1 hour. Stir in chili beans; continue to cook for 30 minutes.

Yields 10 to 12 servings

Herbed Crown Roast Of Pork With Savory Pilaf

1/2 CUP VEGETABLE OIL
1 TEASPOON DRIED ROSEMARY, CRUSHED
1 TEASPOON DRIED THYME, CRUSHED
1/2 TEASPOON RUBBED SAGE
1/2 TEASPOON PAPRIKA
4 CLOVES GARLIC, MINCED
1 14- TO 16-RIB CROWN ROAST (ABOUT 7 POUNDS)
SALT AND PEPPER TO TASTE

Mix together oil, rosemary, thyme, sage, paprika and garlic in small bowl. Season meat with salt and pepper. Brush meat with seasoned oil mixture. Place meat, bone-end up, in shallow roasting pan; wrap bone ends with aluminum foil to prevent excessive browning. To hold shape, place a small ovenproof bowl or souffle dish in center of roast; secure with string. Insert meat thermometer so that tip is in center of thickest part of meat and does not rest on fat or bone. Roast in 325-degree oven for 17 minutes per pound (about 2 hours for a 7-pound roast), brushing with oil mixture occasionally. Transfer roast to heated platter; drain drippings from pan, reserving 1/4 cup for gravy. Tent with foil and let stand 20 minutes. Remove bowl from center of roast and discard foil and string. Spoon Savory Pilaf into center.

Yields 8 servings

SAVORY PILAF

1/3 CUP UNCOOKED BROWN RICE
1 1/2 CUPS UNSALTED CHICKEN BROTH
1/3 CUP THIN SPAGHETTI, BROKEN INTO 1/2- TO 1-INCH PIECES
2 TEASPOONS REDUCED-CALORIE MARGARINE
2 TABLESPOONS SLICED GREEN ONION
2 TABLESPOONS CHOPPED GREEN PEPPER
1 CLOVE GARLIC, MINCED
1/2 TEASPOON THYME
1/4 TEASPOON SALT

1/8 TEASPOON PEPPER

2 TABLESPOONS CHOPPED PARSLEY

Cook rice in 1 cup of the broth in a covered saucepan until almost tender, about 25 minutes. Cook spaghetti in margarine over low heat until golden brown, about 2 minutes. Stir frequently; watch carefully. Add browned spaghetti, onions, green pepper, garlic, thyme, salt, pepper and remaining 1/2 cup broth to rice. Bring to a boil; reduce heat and cover. Cook over medium heat until liquid is absorbed, about 10 minutes. Remove from heat; let stand 2 minutes. Garnish with parsley.

Yields 6 servings

Braised Pork Chops And Apples

4 TO 6 PORK CHOPS (ABOUT 3/4- TO 1-INCH THICK)

1 TABLESPOON OLIVE OIL

1/2 TEASPOON SALT

1/2 TEASPOON PEPPER

1/2 CUP CHICKEN BROTH OR DRY WHITE WINE

1/2 TEASPOON DRIED THYME, CRUSHED

4 ROME BEAUTY APPLES OR OTHER COOKING APPLES, CORED AND SLICED

2 TABLESPOONS CHOPPED PARSLEY

Brown pork chops in oil on both sides until golden brown in large skillet. Pour off drippings. Sprinkle chops with salt and pepper. Add broth and thyme; reduce heat to low. Cover and simmer for 50 minutes, spooning pan liquid over chops occasionally. Add apples. Cover and cook 5 to 10 minutes or until done. Garnish with parsley if desired.

Yields 4 to 6 servings

Veal Chops With Mushrooms And Onions

2 TEASPOONS OLIVE OIL

1 LARGE ONION, THINLY SLICED

2 CUPS SLICED MUSHROOMS

2 CLOVES GARLIC, THINLY SLICED

4 VEAL LOIN CHOPS 1/2-INCH THICK, ABOUT 4 TO 5 OUNCES EACH

1 TEASPOON DRIED SAGE, CRUSHED

SALT AND PEPPER TO TASTE

1/4 CUP CHICKEN BROTH

1 TABLESPOON DRY RED WINE

2 TABLESPOONS CHOPPED PARSLEY

Heat olive oil over medium heat in large skillet; add onion, mushrooms and garlic. Cook and stir until onion is tender and mushrooms are light brown. Remove vegetables to a serving platter and keep warm. Sprinkle veal chops with half of the sage, salt and pepper. Place chops in same skillet and cook over medium-high heat for 3 minutes on each side, or until done. Remove the chops to a serving platter. Add chicken broth and wine to pan juices in skillet. Cook for about 2 to 3 minutes, stirring constantly until the sauce has reduced slightly. Stir in remaining sage. Pour sauce over the veal chops and onions. Garnish with chopped parsley.

Yields 4 servings

Pan Pizza

1   16-OUNCE PACKAGE HOT ROLL MIX

1/2   POUND ITALIAN SAUSAGE, CASING REMOVED AND CRUMBLED

1/4   CUP CHOPPED ONION

1   CLOVE GARLIC, MINCED

1/4   CUP GRATED PARMESAN CHEESE

1   16-OUNCE CAN TOMATOES, CUT-UP

1/3   CUP TOMATO PASTE

1   4-OUNCE CAN MUSHROOM STEMS AND PIECES, DRAINED

1   TEASPOON SUGAR

2   TEASPOONS ITALIAN SEASONING

1/2   TEASPOON FENNEL SEED

1/2   TEASPOON SALT (OPTIONAL)

2   CUPS SHREDDED MOZZARELLA CHEESE

Prepare hot roll mix according to package directions. Knead and cover. With greased fingers pat dough onto bottom and halfway up sides of greased 15x10x1-inch baking pan. Bake in 375-degree oven for 20 to 25 minutes. Cook sausage, onion and garlic over medium heat in large skillet until meat is brown; drain. Stir in Parmesan cheese, tomatoes, tomato paste, mushrooms, sugar, Italian seasoning, fennel and salt. Spread meat mixture over hot baked crust. Sprinkle with Mozzarella cheese. Bake 20 to 25 minutes longer. Let stand 5 minutes before cutting.

Yields 8 to 10 servings

Herbed Hamburgers

1   POUND GROUND BEEF

1/4   CUP DRY BREAD CRUMBS

1/4   CUP FINELY CHOPPED ONION

2   TEASPOONS STEAK SAUCE

1/2   TEASPOON DRIED THYME

1/2   TEASPOON DRIED OREGANO

1/2   TEASPOON DRIED BASIL

1/2   TEASPOON GARLIC POWDER

    SALT AND PEPPER TO TASTE

Mix all ingredients. Shape mixture into 4 patties, each about 1-inch thick. Cook hamburgers over medium heat in large skillet, turning frequently until desired doneness, about 15 minutes for medium.

Yields 4 servings

Jerk Spareribs

1   BUNCH GREEN ONIONS, GREEN ONLY, THINLY SLICED

2   MEDIUM ONIONS, CHOPPED

4   LARGE CLOVES GARLIC, FINELY MINCED

1   TABLESPOON FINELY MINCED FRESH GINGERROOT

1 TO 2 SCOTCH BONNET OR HABANERO CHILES, SEEDED, RIBBED AND FINELY MINCED

1   TABLESPOON GROUND ALLSPICE

1   TEASPOON BLACK PEPPER

1   TABLESPOON RED PEPPER SAUCE

1   TEASPOON GROUND CINNAMON

1/2   TEASPOON GROUND NUTMEG

1   TEASPOON DRIED THYME

1   TEASPOON SALT

1   TABLESPOON DARK BROWN SUGAR

1/2   CUP ORANGE JUICE

1/2   CUP RICE VINEGAR

1/4   CUP RED-WINE VINEGAR

1/4   CUP SOY SAUCE

1/4   CUP OLIVE OR VEGETABLE OIL

5 TO 6 POUNDS PORK SPARERIBS

Combine green onion, onion, garlic, gingerroot and chile in bowl; Reserve. Combine allspice, black pepper, red pepper sauce, cinnamon, nutmeg, thyme, salt and sugar in another bowl; mix thoroughly. Whisk in orange juice, vinegars and soy sauce. Slowly drizzle in oil, whisking constantly. Add the reserved green onion mix; stir to combine. Let stand at least one hour. Put the ribs in large glass baking dish or bowl and pour the marinade over them, turning them to make certain they are coated on both sides. Refrigerate covered for at least 5 hours or overnight (preferably overnight).

Heat oven to 350 degrees. Place ribs in a large roasting pan. Brush them with some of the marinade. Bake, uncovered, until they are cooked through, about 2 hours. Baste occasionally and turn to ensure even cooking.

NOTE: Ribs can be cooked on grill.

Yields 6 servings

Lamb Curry

1/3	CUP ALL-PURPOSE FLOUR
	SALT AND PEPPER TO TASTE
1/2	TEASPOON PAPRIKA
2 1/2	POUNDS BONELESS LEG OF LAMB, WELL-TRIMMED AND CUT INTO 1 1/2-INCH CUBES
3	TABLESPOONS VEGETABLE OIL
1	LARGE ONION, CHOPPED
1	LARGE GREEN PEPPER, CHOPPED
2	LARGE CLOVES GARLIC, MINCED
2	TABLESPOONS CURRY POWDER
1/4	TEASPOON CRUSHED RED PEPPER
1	14¼-OUNCE CAN DICED TOMATOES, UNDRAINED
1	CUP CHICKEN BROTH

1	TABLESPOON BROWN SUGAR
	ACCOMPANIMENTS (MANGO CHUTNEY, SHREDDED TOASTED COCONUT, RAISINS AND CHOPPED PEANUTS)

Combine flour, salt, pepper and paprika. Coat lamb cubes with flour mixture; shake off the excess. Heat oil in Dutch oven or large saucepan. Brown lamb cubes in 2 or 3 batches, browning each piece on all sides. Remove to bowl with slotted spoon. Add more oil if necessary. Add onion, green pepper, garlic, curry powder and crushed red pepper. Cook until vegetables are tender, about 5 minutes. Add lamb cubes with juices to pan. Stir in tomatoes, chicken broth and brown sugar. Bring to boil over medium-high heat. Reduce heat to low. Cover and simmer for 1 hour or until the lamb is tender. Serve with cooked rice and accompaniments.

Yields 6 servings

Spicy Grilled Chops

1	TEASPOON SEASONED SALT
1/2	TEASPOON CAYENNE PEPPER
1	TEASPOON RUBBED SAGE
1	TABLESPOON PAPRIKA
1/2	TEASPOON BLACK PEPPER
1/2	TEASPOON GARLIC POWDER
4	BONELESS CENTER PORK LOIN CHOPS, 1 1/2 INCHES THICK

Combine spices and mix well. Coat chops with spice mixture. Grill over medium-high heat 10 to 12 minutes per side, turning once.

Yields 4 servings

Lemon-Herb Leg Of Lamb

4	LARGE CLOVES GARLIC, FINELY MINCED
1	TEASPOON DRIED ROSEMARY, CRUSHED
1	TEASPOON DRIED THYME, CRUSHED
1 1/2	TEASPOONS GRATED LEMON RIND
	SALT AND PEPPER TO TASTE
1/3	CUP FRESH LEMON JUICE
1	BONE-IN LEG OF LAMB, TRIMMED OF EXCESS FAT (ABOUT 8 POUNDS)
2	TABLESPOONS VEGETABLE OIL
1	CUP WATER
2	TABLESPOONS ALL-PURPOSE FLOUR
2	CUPS BEEF BROTH

Heat oven to 450 degrees. Combine garlic, rosemary, thyme and rind in small bowl; stir in 1 tablespoon lemon juice. Cut about 12 deep slits with the tip of a small knife on each side of lamb. Push about 1/4 teaspoon of garlic mixture into each slit. Rub the lamb with the oil, then sprinkle with salt and pepper. Place lamb on rack in a large roasting pan. Pour in water. Roast for 15 minutes. Spoon remaining lemon juice over meat, and reduce the temperature to 350 degrees. Continue to cook for 1½ to 2 hours, basting occasionally with pan juices to desired doneness. Insert meat thermometer in the thickest part of lamb not touching fat or bone (temperature readings for rare is 130 degrees, 140 degrees for medium and 150 degrees for medium well). Remove the lamb to serving platter and cover loosely with foil to keep warm. Let the lamb rest for 15 minutes.

To make gravy, spoon off and discard all but 2 tablespoons of fat from juices in roasting pan. Whisk in the flour until smooth, scraping up the browned bits from the bottom of the pan. Gradually whisk in the beef broth until blended. Heat pan over medium-high heat. Bring to a boil, reduce heat to low and simmer for 5 minutes, stirring until the gravy is thickened. Season with salt and pepper if needed. Serve gravy with lamb.

Yields 12 servings

Jamaican Ground Meat Pita Sandwiches

4	PITA BREADS, HALVED
1	POUND LEAN GROUND SIRLOIN
1	SMALL ONION, FINELY CHOPPED
1/2	TEASPOON MINCED SCOTCH BONNET OR JALAPEÑO PEPPER
	SALT AND PEPPER TO TASTE
1 1/4	TEASPOONS CURRY POWDER
1 1/4	TEASPOONS DRIED THYME
1	TEASPOON GROUND CUMIN
1/4	TEASPOON GROUND ALLSPICE
2	TABLESPOONS BEEF BROTH OR TOMATO JUICE

Cut each pita bread in half; set aside. Cook and stir beef in large skillet until brown. Add onion and Scotch bonnet pepper and cook until onion is tender, about 5 minutes. Add salt, pepper, curry powder, thyme, cumin and allspice. Cook for about 5 minutes; add broth if necessary to keep the mixture moist. Spoon mixture into pita halves and serve immediately.

Yields 4 servings

VEGETABLES & SIDE DISHES

Asparagus With Lemon Mayonnaise

Asparagus With Lemon Mayonnaise

1/2	CUP MAYONNAISE
1	TABLESPOON FRESH LEMON JUICE
1	TEASPOON GRATED LEMON RIND
2	TABLESPOONS MILK
2	POUNDS THIN ASPARAGUS SPEARS

Stir together mayonnaise, lemon juice, lemon rind and milk in small bowl. Keep cold. Trim asparagus. Bring the asparagus to a boil and cook about 2 minutes until crisp-tender. Remove with tongs to strainer and run under cold water until asparagus is cool; drain well. Arrange asparagus on platter and garnish with lemon slices. Serve with Lemon Mayonnaise.

Yields 8 servings

Stir-Fried Asparagus

1	POUND FRESH ASPARAGUS, TRIMMED AND SLICED DIAGONALLY (ABOUT 3 CUPS)
1	SMALL ONION, SLICED
1	SMALL CLOVE GARLIC, MINCED
2	TABLESPOONS BUTTER OR MARGARINE
2	TABLESPOONS SLICED ALMONDS
	GRATED PEEL OF 1/2 LEMON
1	TABLESPOON LEMON JUICE
1/2	TEASPOON LITE SOY SAUCE

Stir-fry asparagus, onion and garlic in butter until just tender in large nonstick skillet, about 5 minutes. Stir in remaining ingredients; heat for 1 to 2 minutes.

Yields 4 servings

Carrots Lyonnaise

6	MEDIUM CARROTS
1	CHICKEN BOUILLON CUBE
1/2	CUP BOILING WATER
2	TABLESPOONS REDUCED-CALORIE MARGARINE
1	MEDIUM ONION, SLICED
1	TABLESPOON ALL-PURPOSE FLOUR
1/4	TEASPOON SALT, OPTIONAL
1/8	TEASPOON PEPPER
1/4	TEASPOON SUGAR

Cut carrots into julienne strips. Dissolve bouillon cube in the 1/2 cup boiling water in 2-quart saucepan; add carrots. Cover and cook over medium heat 10 minutes. Melt butter in 10-inch skillet; add onion. Cover and cook 5 minutes, stirring occasionally. Stir in flour, salt, pepper and sugar. Add carrots and bouillon mixture; simmer uncovered 5 to 10 minutes.

Yields 6 servings

Skillet Greens With Balsamic Vinegar

2	POUNDS COLLARDS, WASHED AND DRAINED
2	CUPS WATER
3	TABLESPOONS BACON DRIPPINGS OR OLIVE OIL
1	SMALL ONION, THINLY SLICED
2	CLOVES GARLIC, MINCED
1/8	TEASPOON CRUSHED RED PEPPER
2 TO 3	TEASPOONS SUGAR
2	TABLESPOONS BALSAMIC VINEGAR

Remove and discard the woody stems. Stack the collard leaves a few at a time and roll. Cut them crosswise into 1/4 inch-wide strips.

Bring water to a boil in Dutch oven or large saucepan. Add collards; cover and cook over medium heat, stirring often until greens are slightly tender, about 10 to 12 minutes. Drain greens well. Heat bacon drippings in large skillet over medium heat until hot. Add onion, garlic and crushed red pepper; cook and stir until onion is tender, about 5 minutes. Add drained collards and sugar, cook and stir until collards are tender, about 10 minutes. Sprinkle balsamic vinegar over collards and toss to coat. Serve immediately.

Yields 6 servings

Calico Broccoli

1	10-OUNCE PACKAGE FROZEN BROCCOLI
1	CUP FROZEN WHOLE KERNEL CORN
1	4-OUNCE CAN MUSHROOM SLICES
1/2	CUP CHOPPED ONION
1/4	CUP CHOPPED RED BELL PEPPER
1/2	CUP WATER
1/2	TEASPOON DRIED BASIL
1/2	TEASPOON INSTANT VEGETABLE BOUILLON
1	CLOVE GARLIC, MINCED
2	TABLESPOONS CHOPPED PARSLEY

Heat all ingredients to boiling; reduce heat. Cover and simmer until vegetables are crisp-tender, 4 to 5 minutes.

Yields 6 servings

Mixed Greens

1	POUND SMOKED TURKEY PARTS
1 1/2	QUARTS WATER
1 OR 2	HOT PEPPER PODS OR 1/4 TEASPOON CRUSHED RED PEPPER
2	LARGE CLOVES GARLIC, MINCED
4	POUNDS FRESH MIXTURE OF GREENS (COLLARDS, TURNIPS, MUSTARD OR KALE)
1 TO 3	TEASPOONS SUGAR
1	TABLESPOON VEGETABLE OIL, OPTIONAL SALT TO TASTE
1	MEDIUM ONION, THICKLY SLICED

Place turkey parts in Dutch oven or large saucepan; add water, pepper pod and garlic. Bring to boil; cover and reduce heat to low and simmer 45 minutes to 1 hour. Meanwhile, break off stems of greens. Wash leaves thoroughly. Slice leaves into bite-size pieces by rolling several leaves together and slicing into 1/4-inch strips. Add greens, sugar, vegetable oil and salt. Cover and cook for about 45 to 55 minutes or until tender. Place sliced onion on top of greens; cover and cook 5 minutes longer.

Yields 8 to 10 servings

Garlic Broccoli And Cauliflower

1   BUNCH BROCCOLI
1   SMALL HEAD CAULIFLOWER
2   TABLESPOONS BUTTER OR MARGARINE
1   LARGE CLOVE GARLIC, CRUSHED
     PEPPER TO TASTE

Trim off leaves; remove tough ends of lower stems. Cut flowerets from central stalks. Peel stalks down to tender interior and cut into pieces. Remove outer leaves and stalk from cauliflower. Cut off any discoloration and separate into flowerets. Heat 1 inch salted water to boiling. Add broccoli and cauliflower. Cover and heat to boiling; reduce heat. Boil until just tender, about 5 minutes. Drain. Heat butter in small saucepan until melted; add garlic. Cook butter mixture 1 to 2 minutes over very low heat. Pour over drained vegetables and toss gently.

Yields 6 servings

Gingered Spinach In Tomato Cups

4   SMALL TOMATOES
2   TEASPOONS FINELY CHOPPED GINGERROOT
2   TEASPOONS VEGETABLE OIL
1   SMALL CLOVE GARLIC, MINCED
1   TEASPOON SOY SAUCE
1   POUND FRESH SPINACH, CLEANED AND STEMS REMOVED
1/2   CUP CHOPPED WATER CHESTNUT, OPTIONAL

Remove 1/4 inch from top of tomato; scoop out seeds and pulp; lightly sprinkle with salt; set aside.

Cook and stir gingerroot in oil in 10-inch skillet over medium heat. Stir in garlic, soy sauce and half of the spinach. Cook and stir until spinach begins to wilt. Stir in remaining spinach and water chestnuts. Cook and stir until spinach is wilted, about 2 minutes longer. Fill tomatoes with spinach mixture. Place in shallow baking dish. Bake tomato cups in 375-degree oven for 10 to 15 minutes.

Yields 4 servings

Skillet Cabbage

1   MEDIUM HEAD GREEN CABBAGE
1   TABLESPOON VEGETABLE OIL
2   LARGE CLOVES GARLIC, MINCED
1/8   TEASPOON CRUSHED RED PEPPER
2 TO 3 TEASPOONS SUGAR
1/4   TEASPOON SALT, OPTIONAL
3   GREEN ONIONS, SLICED

Remove outside leaves; wash cabbage. Cut into wedges; coarsely shred cabbage with knife and discard core. Heat oil in large skillet over medium-high heat until hot. Add cabbage, garlic, red pepper, sugar and salt. Stir-fry 2 minutes (keep vegetables moving in skillet); add onion. Stir-fry 1 minute longer or until vegetables are just tender.

Yields 4 servings

Candied Yams With Brandy

6   MEDIUM YAMS, PEELED
1   CUP PACKED LIGHT BROWN SUGAR
1/4   CUP WATER
1/4   CUP FRESH ORANGE JUICE
1   TEASPOON GROUND NUTMEG
1   TEASPOON GROUND CINNAMON
    SALT TO TASTE
1/4   CUP BRANDY
3   TABLESPOONS BUTTER OR MARGARINE
1/3   CUP CHOPPED TOASTED PECANS

Cut yams into thick slices. Mix together sugar, butter, water, orange juice and spices. Place sliced potatoes in baking dish. Sprinkle with salt. Pour sugar mixture over potatoes and add brandy. Cover and bake in 375-degree oven for 30 minutes, spooning sauce over potatoes occasionally. Uncover and continue to cook 15 minutes longer or until sweet potatoes are done. Sprinkle with toasted pecans.

Yields 6 servings

Sauteed Collard Greens

1   BUNCH COLLARD GREENS, ABOUT 2 POUNDS
2   TABLESPOONS BACON DRIPPINGS
1   MEDIUM ONION, CHOPPED
1   HALF-RIPE, FIRM TOMATO, DICED
    SALT AND PEPPER TO TASTE
    DASH NUTMEG

Break off and discard stems of collards. Wash leaves thoroughly. Slice leaves into bite-size pieces by rolling several leaves together and cutting into 1/4-inch strips. Blanch greens in boiling water for 30 minutes; drain well. Melt drippings in large skillet; add onion and cook until tender. Stir in tomato and cook until just tender. Add greens to onion mixture and stir until well-coated. Cook and stir until tender, about 8 to 10 minutes. Stir in a pinch of nutmeg.

Yields 6 servings

Skillet Cabbage

Garlic New Potatoes

1   POUND SMALL NEW POTATOES (UNPEELED)
1   TABLESPOON BUTTER OR MARGARINE
1   TABLESPOON VEGETABLE OIL
1   TABLESPOON OLIVE OIL
4   LARGE GARLIC CLOVES, MINCED
     SALT AND PEPPER TO TASTE
1/4 CUP CHOPPED PARSLEY

Cook potatoes in lightly salted water until tender, about 15 minutes. Drain and cool. Cut potatoes in quarters and set aside. Melt butter with both oils in large heavy skillet over medium heat. Add potatoes and cook 5 minutes, stirring frequently. Increase heat to high. Cook potatoes until deep golden brown, turning frequently, about 20 minutes. Add garlic, salt, pepper and parsley. Continue to cook and stir for 3 minutes. Serve hot.

Yields 6 servings

Southern Fried Corn

8 TO 10 EARS OF CORN
1/4 CUP BACON DRIPPINGS
2   TABLESPOONS ALL-PURPOSE FLOUR
1   TABLESPOON SUGAR
1   CUP WATER
1/4 CUP MILK
     SALT AND PEPPER TO TASTE

Shuck corn. Wash and remove silk. After cutting the kernels in half with a sharp knife, cut kernel off. (This is called cream style-cutting.) Scrape juice out of corn cob into the corn. Heat drippings in large heavy skillet. Add corn, flour, sugar, water, milk, salt and pepper. Bring mixture to boil, stirring constantly. Reduce heat and simmer uncovered until corn is tender, 20 to 25 minutes, stirring occasionally. If necessary, add a little hot water.

Yields 6 servings

Southern Succotash

1   10-OUNCE PACKAGE FROZEN WHOLE KERNEL CORN
1   10-OUNCE PACKAGE FROZEN BABY LIMA BEANS
1   14½-OUNCE CAN TOMATOES, UNDRAINED AND CUT UP
1/2 CUP CHOPPED ONION
2   TABLESPOONS BUTTER OR MARGARINE
1   TEASPOON SUGAR
1/2 TEASPOON SALT, OPTIONAL
1/4 TEASPOON PEPPER
1   10-OUNCE PACKAGE FROZEN CUT OKRA

Combine corn, lima beans, tomatoes, onion, butter, sugar, salt and pepper in 2-quart saucepan. Cover and bring to a boil; reduce heat and simmer 20 minutes, stirring occasionally. Add okra and cook 10 minutes longer or until okra is done.

Yields 6 servings

Skillet Corn

6   EARS FRESH CORN
1/2 CUP CHOPPED GREEN PEPPER
1/2 CUP CHOPPED ONION
1   CLOVE GARLIC, MINCED
2   TABLESPOONS BUTTER OR MARGARINE
1/4 TEASPOON DRIED BASIL, CRUSHED
1/2 TEASPOON SALT, OPTIONAL

1 TEASPOON SUGAR
1 TOMATO, DICED

Cut enough kernels from corn to measure 3 cups. Cook and stir corn, green pepper, onion and garlic in butter in 10-inch skillet over medium heat until onion is tender, about 10 minutes. Stir in remaining ingredients; reduce heat. Cover and cook until corn is tender, 3 to 5 minutes longer.

Yields 6 servings

Red Rice

2 TABLESPOONS BUTTER OR MARGARINE
1 LARGE ONION, CHOPPED
1 MEDIUM GREEN PEPPER, CHOPPED
1 CUP CONVERTED BRAND RICE
1 14½-OUNCE CAN TOMATOES, UNDRAINED AND CUT UP
1 1/2 CUPS CHICKEN BROTH
1 TEASPOON SALT, OPTIONAL
1/4 TEASPOON PEPPER
2 TO 3 DASHES HOT PEPPER SAUCE
1 TABLESPOON TOMATO PASTE

Melt butter in 1½-quart saucepan. Cook onion and green pepper in butter until tender. Stir in rice; add remaining ingredients and blend lightly. Cover and bring to a boil; reduce heat and cook over low heat until rice is tender and all liquid has been absorbed, about 20 minutes.

Yields 4 servings

Summer Squash Casserole

8 CUPS SLICED YELLOW SQUASH (ABOUT 2 POUNDS)
1 CUP SLICED GREEN ONIONS
1 1/2 CUPS WATER
3 EGGS, SLIGHTLY BEATEN
1/4 CUP BUTTER OR MARGARINE
1/2 CUP EVAPORATED MILK
1 CUP COARSELY CRUSHED SALTINE CRACKERS
  SALT AND PEPPER TO TASTE

TOPPING
1/2 cup coarsely crushed saltine crackers
1 tablespoon butter or margarine, melted
 Paprika (optional)

Heat oven to 375 degrees. Put squash and green onions in a large saucepan with about 1½ cups water. Bring to a boil; reduce heat to medium-low and cook until tender, 10 to 15 minutes, stirring occasionally. Drain. Stir in butter, milk, saltines, salt and pepper. Pour squash mixture into a lightly greased 8x8-inch baking dish. To make topping, toss 1/2 cup saltines with 1 tablespoon butter. Sprinkle topping over casserole. Bake until golden brown, 15 to 20 minutes. Sprinkle with paprika, if desired.

Yields 8 servings

Hopping John (Black-Eyed Peas And Rice)

2	SLICES BACON, DICED
1	MEDIUM ONION
1/2	CUP SLICED CELERY
1	LARGE CLOVE GARLIC, MINCED
1/2	TEASPOON DRIED THYME LEAVES, CRUSHED
1	16-OUNCE PACKAGE FROZEN BLACK-EYED PEAS
3	CUPS WATER
1	CUP RICE
1	TEASPOON SALT, OPTIONAL
1/4	TEASPOON CRUSHED RED PEPPER
	SLICED GREEN ONIONS

Cook diced bacon, onion, celery, garlic and thyme until vegetables are tender. Stir in remaining ingredients. Bring to a boil. Reduce heat; cover and simmer 20 to 25 minutes or until liquid is absorbed and rice is done.

Yields 6 servings

Orange-Raisin Rice

8	CUPS WATER
1	CUP WILD RICE
3	CUPS LONG-GRAIN RICE
1/4	CUP VEGETABLE OIL
2	CUPS CHOPPED ONIONS
2	CLOVES GARLIC, MINCED
1	CUP GOLDEN RAISINS
1/2	CUP CHOPPED WATER CHESTNUTS
1/4	CUP CHOPPED PARSLEY
1	TABLESPOON GRATED ORANGE RIND
1	TEASPOON FRESHLY GROUND BLACK PEPPER

Heat salty water to boiling over high heat in 5-quart saucepan. Place wild rice in sieve and rinse well under running cold water. Add wild rice to boiling water; reduce heat to low; simmer covered 20 minutes. Add long-grain rice, cover and simmer 18 to 20 minutes longer until long-grain rice is tender; remove from heat; drain. Heat oil over medium-high heat in medium skillet. Cook onion and garlic 2 to 3 minutes, stirring frequently until tender. Stir cooked onion mixture, raisins and water chestnuts into rice and let stand 5 minutes. Stir in parsley, orange peel and pepper. Garnish with orange slices if desired. This side dish can be used in place of stuffing.

Yields 12 servings

Whiskey Cranberries

2	CUPS FRESH CRANBERRIES
2	CUPS SUGAR
1	TEASPOON GRATED ORANGE RIND
1/4	CUP WHISKEY
1/4	CUP FINELY CHOPPED PECANS

Heat oven to 300 degrees. Wash cranberries well. Spread them evenly on the bottom of a greased shallow baking dish. Sprinkle evenly with sugar and orange rind. Cover; bake for 1 hour, stirring occasionally. When done, remove the cover and gently stir in whiskey and pecans.

Yields 6 servings

Spinach Stir-Fry

2   POUNDS FRESH SPINACH, CLEANED

2   TABLESPOONS VEGETABLE OIL

1 TO 2 CLOVES GARLIC, FINELY CHOPPED

2   GREEN ONIONS, SLICED

1/4   CUP CHICKEN BROTH

    SALT AND PEPPER TO TASTE

Tear spinach into bite-size pieces. Heat wok or large skillet until hot. Add vegetable oil; rotate to coat sides. Add garlic, spinach and green onions; stir-fry for 2 minutes. Stir in chicken broth, salt and pepper. Cover and cook 1 minute

Yields 4 servings

Orange Yams

1 1/2   POUNDS YAMS OR SWEET POTATOES, PEELED AND CUT IN 1 1/2-INCH CUBES

2/3   CUPS ORANGE JUICE (JUICE FROM ABOUT 3 ORANGES)

1/2   CUP WATER

1/2   CUP BROWN SUGAR

2   TABLESPOONS BUTTER OR MARGARINE

1   TEASPOON VANILLA EXTRACT

1/2   TEASPOON GROUND CINNAMON

1/2   TEASPOON GROUND NUTMEG

    DASH SALT

Place yams in 2-quart saucepan. Add orange juice, water, sugar, butter, vanilla, cinnamon, nutmeg and salt. Bring to a boil; reduce heat to medium and continue to cook for 25 minutes or until yams are done, stirring occasionally. If necessary, increase heat and cook until desired sauce consistency.

Yields 6 servings

Oven Omelet

1/4   CUP BUTTER OR MARGARINE

18   EGGS

1   CUP SOUR CREAM

1   CUP MILK

2   TEASPOONS SALT

1   CUP SHREDDED SWISS CHEESE

1   CUP SHREDDED CHEDDAR CHEESE

1/2   CUP FINELY CHOPPED GREEN PEPPER

3   GREEN ONIONS, VERY THINLY SLICED

1   2-OUNCE JAR DICED PIMIENTO, DRAINED

Heat butter in a 13x9x2 baking dish in a 325-degree oven until melted. Tilt dish to coat bottom with melted butter. Beat eggs, sour cream, milk and salt in large mixer bowl until well-blended. Stir in Swiss cheese, Cheddar cheese, green pepper, green onion and pimiento. Pour into baking dish. Cook uncovered until omelet is set but still moist, 40 to 45 minutes. Cut into squares and garnish with additional pimiento or green pepper if desired.

NOTE: After pouring into baking dish, cover and refrigerate no longer than 24 hours. Cook uncovered in 325-degree oven for 50 to 55 minutes.

Yields 12 servings

Glazed Carrots And Turnips

3   TABLESPOONS BUTTER OR MARGARINE

1   POUND WHITE TURNIPS, PEELED AND CUT INTO **1 1/2**-INCH THIN STRIPS

2   MEDIUM CARROTS, CUT INTO **1 1/2**-INCH THIN STRIPS

1   CUP CHICKEN BROTH

1/2   TEASPOON SALT

1/4   TEASPOON WHITE PEPPER

2   TABLESPOONS SUGAR

2   TABLESPOONS CHOPPED PARSLEY

Melt butter over medium heat in 10-inch skillet. Add turnips and carrots; toss to coat them with butter. Add broth, cover and cook for 6 minutes. Increase heat to high. Season with salt and pepper. Cook uncovered for 10 minutes or until the vegetables are tender and liquid is reduced and syrupy. Sprinkle sugar over vegetables and reduce heat to medium. Cover and cook, shaking the pan to toss vegetables, for about 1 minute or until vegetables are glazed and shiny. Garnish with parsley if desired.

Yields 6 servings

Curried Potatoes

1/4   CUP BUTTER OR MARGARINE

1 1/2   POUNDS SMALL NEW POTATOES, SCRUBBED AND QUARTERED

1 1/2   TEASPOONS CURRY POWDER

1   TEASPOON SUGAR

2   TABLESPOONS WATER

1/2   TEASPOON SALT, OPTIONAL

1/8   TEASPOON WHITE PEPPER

1/4   CUP THINLY SLICED GREEN ONIONS

Melt the butter in 12-inch skillet, preferably non-stick. Add potatoes, cook and stir uncovered over moderate heat about 10 minutes, stirring occasionally. Sprinkle curry powder, sugar and water over potatoes and stir well. Reduce heat; cover and continue to cook the potatoes 10 minutes until they are tender. Stir in green onions, salt and pepper. Cook uncovered until the potatoes are crisp and lightly browned, about 5 minutes more.

Yields 6 servings

FISH & SEAFOOD

Shrimp Creole

Shrimp Creole

2 TABLESPOONS OLIVE OIL
1 LARGE ONION, CHOPPED
1 LARGE GREEN PEPPER, DICED
1/2 MEDIUM RED BELL PEPPER, DICED
1 CELERY RIB, SLICED
2 LARGE CLOVES GARLIC, MINCED
1 28-OUNCE CAN WHOLE TOMATOES, DRAINED AND CUT UP
1 CUP CLAM JUICE
1/2 TEASPOON DRIED THYME
  HOT PEPPER SAUCE TO TASTE
1 BAY LEAF
  SALT AND PEPPER TO TASTE
1 1/2 POUNDS LARGE SHRIMP, PEELED AND DEVEINED
2 TABLESPOONS CHOPPED PARSLEY
  COOKED RICE

Heat oil in large skillet over medium heat. Add onion, green pepper, red bell pepper, celery and garlic; cook and stir until vegetables are tender. Add tomatoes, clam juice, thyme, hot pepper sauce, bay leaf, salt and pepper. Reduce heat to low and cook, stirring occasionally, for 25 minutes or until the sauce is thick. Add shrimp and cook, stirring occasionally, until the shrimp are done and are opaque, about 4 minutes. Serve over hot cooked rice. Garnish with chopped parsley.

Yields 6 servings

Tequila Shrimp

1/3 CUP TEQUILA
2 TABLESPOONS LIME JUICE
2 TABLESPOONS ORANGE JUICE
2 TABLESPOONS VEGETABLE OIL
2 TABLESPOONS MINCED CILANTRO
2 TABLESPOONS HONEY
1/2 TEASPOON GRATED LIME PEEL
1 CLOVE GARLIC, MINCED
  SALT AND PEPPER TO TASTE
1 1/2 POUNDS SHRIMP, SHELLED AND DEVEINED
  LIME
  CILANTRO

Mix together tequila, lime juice, orange juice, oil, cilantro, honey, lime peel and garlic in nonmetal bowl. Pour tequila mixture into large nonstick skillet. Add shrimp. Cook over medium-high heat, stirring until shrimp are just opaque but still moist in center, about 3 to 4 minutes. With a slotted spoon, transfer shrimp to a platter and keep warm. Bring cooking liquid to a boil over high heat. Boil until reduced to 1/3 cup. Season with salt and pepper. Remove pan from heat. Spoon reduced cooking liquid over shrimp. Garnish with limes and cilantro.

Yields 6 servings

Herb-Baked Catfish

2 POUNDS CATFISH FILLETS
2 TABLESPOONS REDUCED-CALORIE MARGARINE, MELTED
1 MEDIUM CLOVE GARLIC, MINCED
  SALT AND PEPPER TO TASTE
3/4 TEASPOON PAPRIKA
1/2 TEASPOON DRIED BASIL, CRUSHED
1/2 TEASPOON DRIED OREGANO, CRUSHED
1/2 TEASPOON DRIED THYME, CRUSHED
2 TABLESPOONS FRESH LEMON JUICE
2 TABLESPOONS CHOPPED PARSLEY

Combine melted margarine and garlic; spread

margarine mixture over bottom of a rectangular 13x8x2-inch pan. Season fish fillets with salt and pepper. Combine paprika, basil, oregano and thyme. Sprinkle herb mixture on both sides of fish. Arrange fish on top of margarine mixture. Drizzle with lemon juice. Bake at 350 degrees for 15 to 18 minutes or until fish is almost done.

Move the baking dish to about 4 to 6 inches from heat and broil 4 to 6 minutes longer or until fish flakes when tested. Remove fish to serving platter and pour pan juices over fish. Sprinkle with chopped parsley.

Yields 6 servings

Oven-Fried Catfish

4   CATFISH FILLETS
1/4   TEASPOON SALT, OPTIONAL
1/4   TEASPOON PEPPER
1/2   TEASPOON GARLIC POWDER
1/4   CUP YELLOW CORNMEAL
1/4   CUP DRY BREAD CRUMBS
1/2   TEASPOON PAPRIKA
2   TABLESPOONS REDUCED-CALORIE MARGARINE

Move oven rack to position slightly above middle of oven. Heat oven to 450 degrees. Season fish with salt, pepper and garlic powder. Combine cornmeal, bread crumbs and paprika. Coat fish with cornmeal mixture. Spray rectangular 13x9x2-inch pan with vegetable cooking spray. Place fish in pan; drizzle with melted margarine. Bake uncovered until fish flakes very easily with fork, 20 to 25 minutes.

Yields 4 servings

Garlicky Catfish Bouillabaisse

1/4   CUP OLIVE OR VEGETABLE OIL
4   MEDIUM ONIONS, CUT INTO 1/4-INCH SLICES
4   LARGE CLOVES GARLIC, THINLY SLICED
5   FISH BOUILLON CUBES
5   CUPS WATER
2   CUPS DRY WHITE WINE
1   16-OUNCE CAN DICED TOMATOES, UNDRAINED
         CAYENNE PEPPER TO TASTE
1/2   TEASPOON SAFFRON THREADS OR 1/2 TEASPOON TURMERIC
1   TEASPOON DRIED THYME
1   BAY LEAF
         SALT AND PEPPER TO TASTE
3   MEDIUM CARROTS, SLICED
2   MEDIUM POTATOES
1 1/2   POUNDS CATFISH FILLETS, CUT INTO CUBES

Over medium heat, heat oil in a large heavy pan or Dutch oven. Add onion and garlic; cook until tender, stirring frequently. Dissolve bouillon cubes in 5 cups of water. Add to onion mixture. Stir in wine, undrained tomatoes, cayenne, saffron, thyme, bay leaf, salt and pepper to taste. Bring to a boil. Reduce heat. Cover and simmer for 5 minutes. Add potatoes and carrots. Cover and simmer until vegetables are tender, about 12 minutes. Add fish. Cover and simmer 10 minutes longer. Remove bay leaf and discard.

Yields 6 servings

Catfish Gumbo

1	POUND CATFISH FILLETS
1/2	CUP CHOPPED CELERY
1/2	CUP CHOPPED GREEN PEPPER
1/2	CUP CHOPPED ONION
2	MEDIUM CLOVES GARLIC, FINELY CHOPPED
2	TABLESPOONS VEGETABLE OIL
2	CUPS CHICKEN BROTH
1	14½-OUNCE CAN WHOLE TOMATOES, UNDRAINED
1	10-OUNCE PACKAGE FROZEN SLICED OKRA
1/4	TEASPOON CRUSHED RED PEPPER
1 TO 2	TEASPOONS GUMBO FILÉ
	SALT AND PEPPER TO TASTE
1 1/2	CUPS HOT RICE

Cut catfish into 1-inch pieces. Cook celery, green pepper, onion and garlic in vegetable oil in Dutch oven until tender. Add broth, tomatoes, okra, crushed red pepper, gumbo filé, salt and pepper. Cover and simmer 20 minutes. Place fish on vegetables. Cover and simmer 15 minutes longer or until fish flakes easily when tested. Serve with hot cooked rice.

Yields 6 servings

Southern Fried Catfish
With Hushpuppies

2	POUNDS PAN-DRESSED CATFISH
1/2	CUP ALL-PURPOSE FLOUR
1/2	CUP YELLOW CORNMEAL
1	TEASPOON SALT
1/2	TEASPOON PEPPER
	VEGETABLE COOKING OIL

Cut fish into serving-size pieces if fillets are large. Combine cornmeal, flour, salt and pepper. Coat fish with cornmeal mixture. Heat oil (1/2-inch) in skillet until hot. Fry fish in hot oil over medium-high heat, turning fish carefully, until brown on both sides, about 10 minutes

Yields 4 to 6 servings

HUSHPUPPIES

1	CUP YELLOW CORNMEAL
3/4	CUP ALL-PURPOSE FLOUR
4	TEASPOONS BAKING POWDER
2	TEASPOONS SUGAR
1	TEASPOON SALT
1/4	TEASPOON GARLIC POWDER
2/3	CUP MILK
1	EGG, WELL-BEATEN
1/4	CUP FINELY CHOPPED ONION
	VEGETABLE OIL

Combine cornmeal, flour, baking powder, sugar, salt and garlic powder in medium bowl. Stir in milk, egg and onion until well-blended. Drop by rounded teaspoonful into deep hot oil (375 degrees). Fry until golden brown, about 3 minutes. Drain on paper towels. Serve hot.

Yields 4 to 6 servings

Grilled Scallops With Orange Vinaigrette

1/4   CUP ORANGE JUICE

2   TABLESPOONS WINE VINEGAR

1/4   CUP OLIVE OIL

1   TEASPOON ORANGE ZEST

1   SMALL CLOVE GARLIC, MINCED

1   TABLESPOON HONEY

    SALT AND PEPPER TO TASTE

1   POUND SEA SCALLOPS

    BIBB LETTUCE

    RED BELL PEPPER STRIPS

Combine orange juice, vinegar, olive oil, orange zest, garlic, honey, salt and pepper in small bowl. Place scallops on skewers and brush lightly with vinaigrette. Heat grill or broiler. Broil or grill scallops until done, about 2 minutes on each side. Arrange lettuce leaves on 4 serving plates. Remove scallops from skewers and arrange scallops on lettuce. Spoon vinaigrette over scallops. Garnish with red bell pepper strips. Serve immediately.

Yields 4 servings

Lobster Hash

4   LOBSTER TAILS

1/4   CUP BUTTER OR MARGARINE

2   TABLESPOONS VEGETABLE OIL

1   POUND NEW POTATOES, COOKED AND CUT INTO 1/2-INCH CUBES

6   GREEN ONIONS, SLICED

1   SMALL RED BELL PEPPER, CHOPPED

1/4   TEASPOON DRIED THYME, CRUSHED

    SALT AND PEPPER TO TASTE

1   TABLESPOON FRESH LEMON JUICE

Heat 2 quarts salty water to boiling. Add lobster tails; cover and heat to boiling. Reduce heat; simmer 15 minutes. When cool, cut through membranes lengthwise. Remove membranes. Remove meat from shells; cut into 1/2-inch pieces. Heat butter and oil in large skillet over medium heat. Spread potatoes, green onions and red bell pepper in skillet. Cook until potatoes are lightly browned, about 5 minutes. Add lobster, thyme, salt and pepper. Cook and stir until lobster is heated through. Drizzle with lemon juice. Serve at once.

Yields 6 servings

Fish Fillets Florentine

1   10-OUNCE PACKAGE FROZEN SPINACH SOUFFLE, THAWED

1/4   CUP THINLY SLICED GREEN ONION

1/8   TEASPOON GARLIC POWDER

4   SOLE OR FLOUNDER FILLETS (ABOUT 1 POUND)

    LEMON JUICE

Heat oven to 350 degrees. Combine spinach souffle, green onion and garlic powder. Spread spinach mixture on fillets; sprinkle with lemon juice. From a narrow end, roll each fillet, jelly-roll fashion; secure with toothpicks. Arrange rolls side-by-side in a 12x8x2-inch baking dish. Bake fillets until fish flakes easily when tested with fork, about 15 minutes. Remove toothpicks and serve.

Yields 4 servings

Grilled Catfish With Pineapple Salsa

2   TABLESPOONS BUTTER OR MARGARINE, MELTED
1   TABLESPOON LEMON JUICE
1/2 TEASPOON GRATED LEMON RIND
1/2 TEASPOON WORCESTERSHIRE SAUCE
6   CATFISH FILLETS

Mix all ingredients except fish fillets. Cover and grill fish about 4 inches from medium coals, turning and brushing occasionally with butter mixture, until fish flakes easily with fork 15 to 25 minutes. Serve with Pineapple Salsa.

PINEAPPLE SALSA

1/2 FRESH PINEAPPLE, PEELED AND DICED
2   MEDIUM TOMATOES, SEEDED AND DICED
1/2 CUP THINLY SLICED GREEN ONIONS
1   JALAPEÑO PEPPER, SEEDED AND FINELY CHOPPED
2   TABLESPOONS CHOPPED CILANTRO
1   TABLESPOON LIME JUICE
1   CLOVE GARLIC, MINCED
1/2 TEASPOON SALT

Mix ingredients together and refrigerate for at least 30 minutes before serving.

Yields 6 servings

Trout Amandine

1   EGG, SLIGHTLY BEATEN
1   CUP MILK
2   POUNDS TROUT
    SALT AND PEPPER TO TASTE

1/2 CUP ALL-PURPOSE FLOUR
1/4 CUP BUTTER OR MARGARINE
1/2 CUP SLIVERED ALMONDS
1/4 CUP FRESH LEMON JUICE
1   TABLESPOON CHOPPED PARSLEY

Combine egg and milk. Season trout with salt and pepper. Dip trout into egg mixture. Drain and coat with flour; shake off excess flour. Heat butter in 10-inch skillet until melted over medium-high heat. Brown trout on both sides until golden brown, about 4 minutes on each side. Remove trout to serving platter. Add almonds to skillet and brown lightly. Add the lemon juice and parsley, heat through and pour over the fish.

Yields 4 servings

Salmon Patties

1   15½-OUNCE CAN SALMON, DRAINED AND FLAKED
1   EGG, BEATEN
1/3 CUP FINELY CHOPPED ONIONS
1/4 CUP CORNMEAL OR DRY BREAD CRUMBS
2   TABLESPOONS FINELY CHOPPED RED OR GREEN
    BELL PEPPER
    DASH HOT PEPPER SAUCE
    VEGETABLE OIL

Mix all ingredients except vegetable oil. Shape salmon mixture into 6 patties. Heat 1½ to 2 inches of oil in heavy skillet until hot. Fry patties, turning once, until lightly browned, about 8 minutes; place patties on paper towel to drain.

Yields 6 servings

Cornmeal-Seared Fish Fillets

4	FIRM-FLESH FISH FILLETS (SUCH AS GROUPER, ORANGE ROUGHY)
2	TABLESPOONS CORNMEAL
1	TABLESPOON ALL-PURPOSE FLOUR
2	TEASPOONS CAJUN SEASONING
1/4	TEASPOON GARLIC POWDER
1	TABLESPOON VEGETABLE OIL
	LEMON WEDGES

Rinse fish fillets; pat dry. Mix cornmeal, flour, Cajun seasoning and garlic powder. Lightly sprinkle cornmeal mixture on both sides of fillets. Heat heavy skillet over high heat until very hot. Add oil; heat briefly. Add fish and cook, turning several times until fish flakes easily with fork or until done, about 8 to 10 minutes. Serve hot with lemon wedges. If desired, garnish with parsley.

Yields 4 servings

Cajun Salmon Steak

1	TEASPOON PAPRIKA
1/2	TEASPOON BLACK PEPPER
1/2	TEASPOON WHITE PEPPER
1	TEASPOON SALT
1/2	TEASPOON CAYENNE
1/2	TEASPOON GARLIC POWDER
1/2	TEASPOON ONION POWDER
1/2	TEASPOON DRIED OREGANO
1/2	TEASPOON DRIED THYME
4	SALMON STEAKS, ABOUT 1/2-INCH THICK
1	TABLESPOON OLIVE OIL
1/4	CUP WATER

Combine all ingredients except salmon, olive oil and water in small bowl. Coat salmon steaks with seasoning mixture on both sides. Let stand 5 minutes. Heat olive oil in large oven-proof skillet over medium-high heat until hot. Brown salmon on both sides until lightly brown, about 2 minutes on each side. Add water. Heat oven to 400 degrees. Place browned salmon in oven until salmon is done, about 10 minutes. Salmon is done when flakes easily with fork.

Yields 4 servings

Shrimp Scampi

16	RAW JUMBO SHRIMP IN SHELL
1/4	CUP BUTTER OR MARGARINE
2	CLOVES GARLIC, CRUSHED
2	TABLESPOONS LEMON JUICE
	SALT AND PEPPER TO TASTE
2	TABLESPOONS CHOPPED PARSLEY

Wash shrimp and remove legs and shells, leaving tails attached. Devein shrimp by making a shallow cut down center back of each shrimp. Open, cut and rinse away exposed vein. Melt butter in a 10-inch skillet over medium heat. Stir in garlic. Cook briefly but do not brown. Add shrimp. Cook and stir shrimp 1 to 2 minutes on each side until shrimp turns pink and flesh is opaque and firm. Pour lemon juice over shrimp. Season with salt and pepper. Place shrimp on plate. Working quickly, raise heat and boil pan juices until syrupy. Stir in parsley. Pour over shrimp. Serve immediately.

Yields 4 servings

Poached Salmon With Cucumber Dill Sauce

4	FRESH/FROZEN SALMON STEAKS OR FILLETS (ABOUT 6 OUNCES EACH)
4	CUPS BOILING WATER
1	CUP WHITE WINE
1/2	LEMON, SLICED
1	SMALL ONION, SLICED
1/4	TEASPOON DRIED DILL WEED
8	WHOLE PEPPERCORNS

Place all ingredients in large skillet (poaching liquid must cover salmon). If necessary, add boiling water to cover salmon. Bring to a boil. Cover; reduce heat and simmer, allowing 10 minutes per inch of thickness of salmon measured at its thickest part or until salmon flakes easily when tested with a fork. Carefully remove from liquid. Cool; chill until ready to serve. Serve with Cucumber Dill Sauce.

CUCUMBER DILL SAUCE

1	CUP PLAIN YOGURT
2/3	CUP PEELED, SEEDED AND FINELY CHOPPED CUCUMBER
2	TEASPOONS LEMON JUICE
1/4	TEASPOON DRIED DILL WEED, CRUSHED

Combine all ingredients; mix well. Chill at least 1 hour before serving.

Yields 4 servings

Creole Fish

	VEGETABLE COOKING SPRAY
1/2	CUP SLICED CELERY
1/2	CUP CHOPPED GREEN PEPPER
1/2	CUP CHOPPED ONION
1	LARGE CLOVE GARLIC, MINCED
1	14 ½-OUNCE CAN TOMATOES, UNDRAINED AND COARSELY CHOPPED
2	TEASPOONS WORCESTERSHIRE SAUCE
2	TEASPOONS FRESH LEMON JUICE
1/2	TEASPOON DRIED THYME, CRUSHED
1/8 TO 1/4	TEASPOON CRUSHED RED PEPPER
1	POUND FISH FILLETS

Spray a large skillet with vegetable cooking spray; place over medium heat until hot. Add celery, green pepper and onion to skillet; cook until vegetables are tender, about 3 to 5 minutes.

Add remaining ingredients except fish to vegetable mixture; bring to boil. Add fish; spoon sauce over fish. Cover; reduce heat and simmer 2 minutes. Uncover and continue to cook until fish flakes easily with fork, 8 to 10 minutes. Serve with rice if desired.

Yields 4 servings

Baked Stuffed Red Snapper

	8- TO 10-POUND CLEANED RED SNAPPER FISH
	VEGETABLE OIL
	SALT AND PEPPER TO TASTE
1	CUP CHOPPED CELERY AND ONION
1	MEDIUM CLOVE GARLIC, CRUSHED
1/4	TEASPOON EACH DRIED ROSEMARY, SAGE AND THYME
1/4	CUP BUTTER OR MARGARINE

3	CUPS DRY BREAD CUBES
1/4	CUP CHOPPED PARSLEY
1	TEASPOON SALT
1	TABLESPOON FRESH LEMON JUICE
1/4	TEASPOON PEPPER
	VEGETABLE OIL
1/2	CUP BUTTER OR MARGARINE, MELTED
1/4	CUP LEMON JUICE

Rub cavity of fish with salt and pepper. Cook and stir celery, onion, and garlic with seasoning in 1/4 cup butter until tender. Gently stir in bread cubes, parsley, 1 teaspoon salt, 1 tablespoon lemon juice, and pepper. Stuff fish cavity with bread crumb mixture. Close opening with skewers or toothpicks. Brush fish with oil; place in shallow roasting pan. Mix 1/2 cup melted butter and 1/4 cup lemon juice together. Bake fish uncovered in 350-degree oven, brushing occasionally with butter mixture until fish flakes very easily with fork, about 1½ hours. Spoon any remaining stuffing into baking dish; refrigerate and bake in oven with fish the last 20 minutes before serving.

Yields 10 servings

Broiled Citrus Catfish Steaks

2	TABLESPOONS FRESH ORANGE JUICE
2	TABLESPOONS FRESH LEMON JUICE
1	TABLESPOON FRESH LIME JUICE
1	TABLESPOON CHILI SAUCE
1/8	TEASPOON ONION POWDER
1	SMALL CLOVE, MINCED
1/2	TEASPOON GRATED ORANGE RIND
2	TEASPOONS HONEY

| | DASH HOT PEPPER SAUCE |
| 8 | 2-OUNCE CATFISH STEAKS |

Combine orange juice, lemon juice, lime juice, chili sauce, onion powder, garlic, orange rind, honey and hot pepper sauce. Pour into a glass dish. Add fish steaks; spread mixture over all surfaces and marinate in refrigerator for at least 1 hour, turning occasionally. Arrange catfish on broiler rack. Broil 4 to 5 inches from heat for 6 minutes; turn fish and brush with remaining marinade. Broil 5 to 6 minutes longer or until fish flakes when tested. Garnish with lemons, limes or oranges if desired.

Yields 4 servings

Herb-Baked Catfish

▼ ▼ ▼ ▼ ▼ ▼ ▼ ▼ ▼ ▼ ▼ ▼ ▼ ▼ ▼ ▼ ▼

Marinated Catfish

1	TABLESPOON VEGETABLE OIL
1/4	CUP DRY WHITE WINE
1	TEASPOON GRATED LEMON RIND
2	TABLESPOONS FRESH LEMON JUICE
2	TABLESPOONS CHOPPED PARSLEY
1	TEASPOON DRIED THYME, CRUSHED
1/2	TEASPOON PAPRIKA
1/2	TEASPOON SALT, OPTIONAL
1/2	TEASPOON GARLIC POWDER
2	POUNDS CATFISH FILLETS

Combine oil, wine, lemon rind, juice, parsley, thyme, paprika, salt and garlic powder in 13x9x2-inch rectangular dish. Place fish in marinade, turning to coat. Marinate 30 minutes.

Arrange fish fillets in shallow baking pan. Bake uncovered at 350 degrees for 20 to 25 minutes or until fish flakes easily when tested with fork, basting frequently with marinade.

Yields 6 servings

PASTAS

▼▼▼▼▼▼▼▼▼▼▼▼▼▼▼▼▼▼

Angel Hair Pasta With Tomatoes and Garlic

Angel Hair Pasta With Tomatoes and Garlic

1	POUND ANGEL HAIR PASTA
2	TABLESPOONS OLIVE OIL
4 TO 5	LARGE CLOVES GARLIC, MINCED
1/8	TEASPOON CRUSHED RED PEPPER
4	CUPS DICED PLUM TOMATOES (ABOUT 8)
1	TEASPOON SUGAR
1/4	CUP SHREDDED FRESH BASIL
	SALT AND PEPPER TO TASTE
	GRATED PARMESAN CHEESE

Cook angel hair pasta as directed on package and drain. Heat olive oil with minced garlic and crushed red pepper over medium heat; cook and stir until garlic is tender, about 2 to 3 minutes. Add tomatoes and sugar and continue to cook until tomatoes are soft, stirring occasionally, about 8 to 10 minutes. Stir in shredded basil. Place cooked pasta in large bowl; pour tomato mixture over pasta and toss to coat pasta. Serve with grated Parmesan cheese.

Yields 4 to 6 servings

Spinach Manicotti

8 TO 10	RAW MANICOTTI SHELLS
2	CUPS RICOTTA CHEESE (1 PINT)
1	10-OUNCE PACKAGE FROZEN, CHOPPED SPINACH, THAWED AND WELL-DRAINED
1	EGG, SLIGHTLY BEATEN
1/2	CUP GRATED PARMESAN CHEESE
1/4	CUP SLICED GREEN ONIONS
1	CLOVE GARLIC, MINCED
	SALT AND PEPPER TO TASTE

2	6-OUNCE CANS ITALIAN TOMATO PASTE
1 1/3	CUPS WATER
3/4	CUP SHREDDED MOZZARELLA CHEESE

Cook manicotti shells as directed on package; drain. Combine ricotta cheese, spinach, egg, Parmesan cheese, onions, garlic, salt and pepper until thoroughly mixed. Fill manicotti shells with spinach mixture. Place manicotti in a 12x7½x2-inch baking dish. Combine Italian tomato paste and water. Pour over manicotti. Sprinkle Mozzarella cheese over top. Bake at 350 degrees for 30 minutes or until sauce is bubbly and heated through.

Yields 4 servings

Marinated Tomatoes And Pasta

3	CUPS CHOPPED TOMATOES (ABOUT 3 MEDIUM)
3	GREEN ONIONS, THINLY SLICED
2	CLOVES GARLIC, FINELY CHOPPED
1/4	CUP CHOPPED FRESH PARSLEY
1/2	TEASPOON SALT
1	TEASPOON DRIED ITALIAN SEASONING
1/4	TEASPOON PEPPER
1	TEASPOON SUGAR
2	TABLESPOONS OLIVE OIL
1	7-OUNCE PACKAGE ANY BITE-SIZE PASTA

Combine tomatoes, onions, garlic, parsley, salt, Italian seasoning, pepper, sugar and oil. Cover and refrigerate at least 2 hours but no longer than 24 hours. Cook pasta as directed on package; drain. Immediately toss with tomato mixture.

Yields 4 servings

Vegetable Pasta Salad

6   OUNCES UNCOOKED MOSTACCIOLI PASTA
2   MEDIUM TOMATOES, CHOPPED
1/2   CUP CRUMBLED FETA CHEESE
1/3   CUP LOW-CALORIE ITALIAN SALAD DRESSING
1/4   CUP THINLY SLICED CELERY
1/4   CUP THINLY SLICED GREEN ONIONS
2   TABLESPOONS SLICED PITTED RIPE OLIVES
6   CUPS TORN FRESH SPINACH
1   TABLESPOON FRESH ORANGE JUICE

Cook pasta according to package directions, then drain. Combine pasta, tomato, cheese, salad dressing, orange juice, green onion, celery and olives. Toss gently to coat. Cover and chill. Toss with spinach just before serving.

Yields 8 servings

Marinara Sauce For Pasta

1   TABLESPOON OLIVE OIL
2   LARGE CLOVES GARLIC, MINCED
1   MEDIUM ONION, FINELY CHOPPED
1   28-OUNCE CAN CRUSHED TOMATOES
1/2   CUP DRY RED WINE
1/2   TEASPOON DRIED THYME
1   TEASPOON DRIED BASIL, CRUSHED
1/2   TEASPOON DRIED MARJORAM, CRUSHED
1/4   TEASPOON DRIED OREGANO , CRUSHED
1/4   TEASPOON CRUSHED RED PEPPER
1/8   TEASPOON PEPPER
      SALT AND PEPPER TO TASTE
      PINCH SUGAR

Heat the oil over low heat in heavy-bottom saucepan. Add garlic and onion and cook until tender, about 10 minutes. Keep heat low and take care not to burn mixture. Add remaining ingredients to saucepan. Simmer, covered for 1 hour on lowest possible heat, stirring frequently. Serve with your favorite pasta.

Yields 3 cups sauce

Spinach Manicotti

Angel Hair Pasta With Shrimp And Herbs

8   OUNCES ANGEL HAIR PASTA
4   TABLESPOONS VEGETABLE OIL
2   TABLESPOONS BUTTER OR MARGARINE
1   POUND RAW SHRIMP, SHELLED AND DEVEINED
3   CLOVES GARLIC, MINCED
1   TABLESPOON FRESH LEMON JUICE
2   TABLESPOONS CHOPPED FRESH BASIL OR 1 1/2 TEA SPOONS DRIED BASIL
2   TABLESPOONS CHOPPED FRESH MARJORAM OR 1 1/2 TEASPOONS DRIED MARJORAM
2   TABLESPOONS CHOPPED PARSLEY
     SALT AND PEPPER TO TASTE
     GRATED PARMESAN CHEESE

Cook the pasta according to package directions until tender but still firm; drain. Heat oil and butter in large skillet until butter is melted. Cook shrimp and garlic until shrimp just turn pink, about 3 to 4 minutes. Stir in lemon juice and herbs. Gently toss the pasta with shrimp mixture until all the strands are coated. Season with salt and pepper. Serve with grated Parmesan cheese. Serve at once.

Yields 4 servings

Lemon Chicken And Spaghetti

2   BONELESS CHICKEN BREASTS, SKINNED
1/4 TEASPOON GARLIC POWDER
     SALT AND PEPPER
1/2 CUP ALL-PURPOSE FLOUR
1/4 TEASPOON PAPRIKA
2   TABLESPOONS VEGETABLE OIL
3   TABLESPOONS BUTTER OR MARGARINE
2   TABLESPOONS FRESH LEMON JUICE
     HOT COOKED SPAGHETTI
     CHOPPED PARSLEY
     GRATED PARMESAN CHEESE

Cut chicken breast into halves. Place each half between two pieces of wax paper; pound until 1/4-inch thick. Sprinkle chicken evenly with garlic powder salt and pepper. Combine flour and paprika. Coat with flour mixture. Heat oil and 2 tablespoons butter in large skillet over medium heat until hot. Cook chicken until done and light brown, about 4 minutes on each side. Remove chicken to warm platter. Heat remaining butter in same skillet until melted. Stir in lemon juice; pour over chicken. Garnish with parsley and lemon slices if desired. Serve with spaghetti and Parmesan cheese.

Yields 4 servings

Spinach-Spaghetti Bake

1   16-OUNCE PACKAGE SPAGHETTI
2   10-OUNCE PACKAGES CHOPPED SPINACH, THAWED AND DRAINED
1   15-OUNCE CONTAINER RICOTTA CHEESE
3   EGGS
1/2 CUP GRATED PARMESAN CHEESE
2   GREEN ONIONS, THINLY SLICED
1/4 TEASPOON PEPPER
1/8 TEASPOON GROUND NUTMEG
1   27-OUNCE JAR SPAGHETTI SAUCE
1   TEASPOON DRIED BASIL, CRUSHED
1/2 TEASPOON DRIED OREGANO, CRUSHED
1   12-OUNCE PACKAGE SHREDDED, LIGHT,

PART-SKIM MOZZARELLA CHEESE

Cook spaghetti as directed on package; drain. Combine spinach, ricotta, eggs, Parmesan cheese, green onions, pepper and nutmeg in medium bowl. Heat oven to 375 degrees. Combine spaghetti, spaghetti sauce, basil and oregano in large bowl. Place half of the spaghetti mixture in a 12x8-inch baking dish. Spoon spinach mixture over spaghetti; sprinkle with half of Mozzarella cheese. Top with remaining spaghetti mixture. Cover and bake 25 minutes or until hot and bubbly. Sprinkle with remaining cheese and bake 5 minutes longer until cheese melts. Let stand 10 minutes before serving.

Yields 8 servings

Ratatouille And Linguine

1	MEDIUM EGGPLANT, PEELED AND CUBED
2	SMALL ZUCCHINI, CUBED
2	SMALL YELLOW SQUASH, CUBED
1	MEDIUM GREEN OR RED BELL PEPPER, DICED
1	MEDIUM ONION, CHOPPED
6 TO 9	PLUM TOMATOES, DICED
2	TABLESPOONS OLIVE OIL
2 TO 3	CLOVES GARLIC, MINCED
1	TEASPOON DRIED BASIL, CRUSHED
1/2	TEASPOON DRIED OREGANO, CRUSHED
1	15-OUNCE JAR SPAGHETTI SAUCE
	COOKED LINGUINE, DRAINED
	GRATED PARMESAN CHEESE

Cook eggplant, zucchini, yellow squash, green pepper, onion, tomatoes in oil with garlic, basil and oregano until tender, about 10 minutes. Stir in spaghetti sauce and continue to cook over low heat until vegetables are done, about 10 minutes. Serve over cooked linguine. Sprinkle with grated Parmesan cheese if desired.

Yields 6 to 8 servings

Pasta And Shrimp Salad

1	8-OUNCE PACKAGE SHELL PASTA OR OTHER SHAPE PASTA
1	CUP CHOPPED CELERY
1/2	CUP CHOPPED GREEN PEPPER
1/4	CUP CHOPPED PIMIENTO
1	POUND CLEANED, COOKED SHRIMP
1/2	CUP MAYONNAISE
1	TABLESPOON FRESH LEMON JUICE
1/2	CUP SOUR CREAM
	SALT AND PEPPER TO TASTE
1/4	CUP CHOPPED PARSLEY

Cook pasta according to package directions; drain and rinse in cold water. Combine cold pasta with celery, green pepper, pimiento and shrimp. Blend mayonnaise, lemon juice, sour cream, salt and pepper; add to pasta mixture, and toss to combine ingredients. Chill several hours. Just before serving, garnish with parsley.

Yields 4 to 6 servings

Vegetable Lasagna

1/3	CUP BUTTER OR MARGARINE
1/3	CUP ALL-PURPOSE FLOUR
1	TEASPOON SALT, OPTIONAL
1/8	TEASPOON GROUND NUTMEG
3	CUPS MILK
1	10-OUNCE PACKAGE FROZEN CHOPPED SPINACH, THAWED AND THOROUGHLY DRAINED
2	CUPS RICOTTA CHEESE
1/2	CUP GRATED PARMESAN CHEESE
1	TEASPOON DRIED BASIL, CRUSHED
1	TEASPOON DRIED OREGANO, CRUSHED
1/2	TEASPOON GARLIC POWDER
1/4	TEASPOON PEPPER
12	LASAGNA NOODLES, COOKED AND DRAINED
1 1/2	CUPS SHREDDED MOZZARELLA CHEESE
1	8-OUNCE CAN SLICED MUSHROOMS, DRAINED
2	MEDIUM CARROTS, COARSELY SHREDDED
1	MEDIUM ONION, CHOPPED
1	MEDIUM GREEN PEPPER, CHOPPED

To make white sauce, heat butter in 1-quart saucepan over low heat until melted. Stir in flour, salt and nutmeg. Cook over low heat, stirring constantly, until bubbly; remove from heat. Stir in milk. Heat to boiling, stirring constantly. Boil and stir 1 minute; cover and keep warm (if sauce thickens, beat in small amount of milk).

Mix spinach, ricotta cheese, 1/4 cup of the Parmesan cheese, the basil, oregano, garlic powder and pepper. Arrange 4 noodles in an ungreased 13x9x2-inch baking dish. Top with half the cheese mixture, 1/2 cup of Mozzarella cheese, 1/2 cup white sauce and 4 noodles. Layer mushrooms, carrots, onion and green pepper on top. Pour on 1/2 cup white sauce and sprinkle with 1/2 cup of the mozzarella cheese. Top with remaining noodles, cheese mixture, white sauce and mozzarella cheese; sprinkle with remaining 1/4 cup Parmesan cheese. Cook lasagna uncovered in 350-degree oven until hot and bubbly, about 35 minutes. Let stand 10 minutes before serving.

Yields 8 servings

Grilled Chicken And Penne Salad

1	POUND SKINNED, BONELESS CHICKEN BREAST HALVES
	SALT AND PEPPER TO TASTE
1/4	CUP LEMON JUICE
1/2	POUND PENNE PASTA, COOKED AS DIRECTED ON PACKAGE, DRAINED
3	MEDIUM PLUM TOMATOES, CHOPPED
1/2	CUP SHREDDED MOZZARELLA CHEESE
1/2	CUP SLICED RIPE OLIVES
1	TEASPOON ITALIAN SEASONING
	LITE ITALIAN SALAD DRESSING
1	CUP COARSELY CHOPPED SALAD GREENS

Season chicken with salt and pepper. Grill or broil until done and chicken is no longer pink, basting with lemon juice. Slice into 2-inch strips. Combine penne, chicken, tomatoes, Mozzarella cheese, olives and Italian seasoning in large bowl; mix well. Add Italian salad dressing; mix well. Cover; chill. Stir in salad greens. Serve with Parmesan cheese. Refrigerate leftovers.

Yields 4 to 6 servings

Tex-Mex Spaghetti

1	POUND GROUND BEEF
1	CUP CHOPPED ONION
1/2	CUP CHOPPED GREEN PEPPER
2	LARGE CLOVES GARLIC, MINCED
2	TABLESPOONS CHILI POWDER
1	TEASPOON DRIED OREGANO
1/4	TEASPOON GROUND CUMIN
1	16-OUNCE CAN CHILI BEANS, UNDRAINED
1	16-OUNCE CAN TOMATOES, UNDRAINED AND CUT UP
1	8-OUNCE CAN TOMATO SAUCE
2	TEASPOONS SUGAR
	SALT AND PEPPER TO TASTE
1/4 TO 1/2	TEASPOON CRUSHED RED PEPPER
	COOKED SPAGHETTI
	SHREDDED CHEDDAR CHEESE

Cook and stir ground beef, onion and green pepper in 3-quart saucepan until beef is brown; drain. Stir in remaining ingredients except spaghetti and cheese. Heat to boiling; reduce heat. Cover and simmer, stirring occasionally, about 30 minutes or until desired consistency. Serve over cooked spaghetti and garnish with shredded cheese if desired.

Yields 4 to 6 servings

Confetti Orzo

2	CUPS ORZO (RICE-SHAPED PASTA)
1	SMALL ZUCCHINI, DICED
1/2	SMALL RED BELL PEPPER, DICED
1/2	SMALL YELLOW BELL PEPPER, DICED
3	CLOVES GARLIC, MINCED
1	TABLESPOON CHOPPED FRESH BASIL
2	TABLESPOONS OLIVE OIL
4	GREEN ONIONS, DIAGONALLY SLICED
1/4	CUP SLICED BLACK OLIVES
	SALT AND PEPPER TO TASTE

Cook orzo until al dente (just tender) in boiling salted water; drain well. Cook and stir zucchini, red bell pepper, yellow bell pepper, garlic and basil in oil in large skillet until vegetables are just tender, about 4 minutes. Add orzo and continue to cook until heated through. Stir in green onions, olives, salt and pepper. Garnish with fresh basil if desired.

Yields 8 servings

Italian Seafood Sauce And Spaghetti

1	TABLESPOON BUTTER OR MARGARINE
1/4	CUP THINLY SLICED CELERY
1	CLOVE GARLIC, MINCED
1	15 ½-OUNCE JAR SPAGHETTI SAUCE
1/4	CUP DRY WHITE WINE
1/2	POUND BAY SCALLOPS
1/2	POUND MEDIUM SHRIMP, CLEANED AND DEVEINED
	HOT COOKED SPAGHETTI
	CHOPPED PARSLEY

Melt butter in 2-quart saucepan over medium heat; cook celery and garlic until tender. Stir in spaghetti sauce, wine, scallops and shrimps. Heat to boiling. Reduce heat to low; cover. Simmer 5 minutes or until shrimp are pink and opaque. Serve hot over spaghetti. Garnish with parsley.

Yields 4 servings

Pasta With Prosciutto And Sun-Dried Tomatoes

2   TABLESPOONS BUTTER OR MARGARINE
3   TABLESPOONS OLIVE OIL
4   CLOVES GARLIC, MINCED
    DASH CRUSHED RED PEPPER
1/4 POUND THINLY SLICED PROSCIUTTO, CUT INTO THIN STRIPS
1/2 CUP DRAINED SUN-DRIED TOMATOES, CUT INTO VERY THIN STRIPS
1/4 CUP CHOPPED FRESH BASIL
1   POUND ANGEL HAIR PASTA, COOKED AND DRAINED
    GRATED PARMESAN CHEESE

Melt butter with oil in large heavy skillet over medium-low heat. Add garlic and crushed red pepper and cook until garlic is golden, stirring frequently, 1 to 2 minutes. Stir in prosciutto and cook 2 minutes. Add tomatoes and basil. Increase heat and bring to gentle boil. Place pasta in large serving bowl. Pour sauce over and toss thoroughly. Serve with Parmesan cheese.

Yields 4 servings

Easy Linguine Primavera

16   OUNCES LINGUINE
1/4 CUP BUTTER OR MARGARINE
1/4 CUP OLIVE OIL
4   GREEN ONIONS, THINLY SLICED
4   CLOVES GARLIC, MINCED
4   SMALL CARROTS, THINLY SLICED
3   LARGE RIPE TOMATOES, CHOPPED
2   CUPS BROCCOLI FLOWERETS
1 1/2 CUPS SLICED FRESH MUSHROOMS
1/4 CUP CHOPPED FRESH BASIL
     SALT AND PEPPER TO TASTE
     GRATED PARMESAN CHEESE

Cook the linguine according to package directions until tender but still firm; drain. Heat butter and oil in large skillet until butter is melted. Cook green onions and garlic until onions are tender. Add the vegetables and cook until they are heated through but still crisp, about 5 to 6 minutes. Add basil to vegetable mixture and toss linguine with vegetable mixture in large bowl. Season with salt and pepper. Serve with grated Parmesan cheese.

Yields 6 servings

BREADS

Centerpiece Citrus Rolls

77

Centerpiece Citrus Rolls

3 1/2 TO 4 CUPS ALL-PURPOSE FLOUR
2   TABLESPOONS SUGAR
1   PACKAGE RAPIDRISE YEAST
3/4   TEASPOON SALT
3/4   CUP WATER
1/2   CUP MILK
1/4   CUP BUTTER OR MARGARINE
1/4   CUP INSTANT POTATO FLAKES OR BUDS
1/2   TEASPOON GRATED LEMON RIND
1/2   TEASPOON GRATED ORANGE RIND
2   EGGS

Combine 1 cup flour, sugar, undissolved yeast and salt in large bowl. Heat water, milk and butter until very warm (120° to 130°). Stir in potato flakes, lemon and orange rind; let soften 1 minute. Stir into dry ingredients. Stir in 1 egg and enough remaining flour to make soft dough. Knead on lightly floured surface until smooth and elastic, about 4 to 6 minutes. Cover; let rest on floured surface 10 minutes.

Divide dough into 12 equal pieces. Roll each piece to 12-inch rope. Coil each rope to make "snail" shape. Arrange rolls in a circle on large greased baking sheet with sides barely touching. Place shallow pan on counter; half fill with boiling water. Place baking sheet on pan. Cover; let rise 15 minutes.

Lightly beat remaining egg; brush over rolls. Bake at 375 degrees until done, about 25 minutes. Remove from sheet; let cool on wire rack.

Yields 1 dozen rolls

Virginia Ham Biscuits

2   CUPS ALL-PURPOSE FLOUR
2   TEASPOONS BAKING POWDER
1/4   TEASPOON SALT
1/4   CUP VEGETABLE SHORTENING
1/2   CUP FINELY GROUND COUNTRY HAM
3/4   CUP BUTTERMILK

Sift together flour, baking powder and salt in deep bowl. Cut shortening and ham into flour mixture with pastry blender until mixture resembles fine crumbs. Stir in buttermilk until dough leaves side of bowl. Turn dough onto lightly floured surface. Knead gently until smooth, about a minute. Roll dough into 1/2 inch thick circle or rectangle; cut with biscuit cutter dipped in flour and place dough on greased baking sheet. Bake in 425-degree oven until golden brown, about 15 to 20 minutes.

Makes about 1½ dozen biscuits

Cornmeal Crescent Rolls

2   PACKAGES ACTIVE DRY YEAST
1/2   CUP WARM WATER (105° TO 115°)
1 1/2 CUPS LUKEWARM MILK (SCALD THEN COOL)
1   CUP YELLOW CORNMEAL
3/4   CUP SUGAR
1/2   CUP BUTTER OR MARGARINE, SOFTENED
2   EGGS, SLIGHTLY BEATEN
2   TEASPOONS SALT
5 3/4 TO 6 1/4 CUPS ALL-PURPOSE FLOUR
       CORNMEAL

Dissolve yeast in warm water. Stir in milk, 1 cup

cornmeal, sugar, 1/2 cup butter, eggs, salt and 2 cups of flour. Beat until smooth. Stir in enough extra flour to make dough easy to handle.

Turn dough onto lightly floured surface; knead until smooth and elastic, about 5 minutes. Place in greased bowl; turn greased bowl; turn greased-side up. Cover; let rise in warm place until doubled, about 1½ hours. (Dough is ready if indentation remains when touched.)

Grease 2 baking sheets; lightly sprinkle with cornmeal. Punch down dough; divide in half. Roll each half into 12-inch circle. Spread with softened butter; cut each circle into 16 wedges. Roll up each wedge, beginning at rounded side. Place crescents with points down on baking sheets. Cover; let rise until doubled, about 40 minutes.

Heat oven to 400 degrees. Brush crescents lightly with melted butter; sprinkle with cornmeal. Bake until golden brown, 15 to 20 minutes.

Yields 32 rolls

Buttermilk Biscuits

3	CUPS SELF-RISING FLOUR
1/4	TEASPOON BAKING POWDER
1/8	TEASPOON BAKING SODA
1	TEASPOON SUGAR
1	CUP VEGETABLE SHORTENING
1	CUP BUTTERMILK

Sift together dry ingredients; cut shortening into flour mixture with pastry blender until mixture resembles fine crumbs. Stir in buttermilk and mix into a soft dough. Turn dough onto floured surface; knead gently until smooth, about a minute. Roll dough into 1/4- to 1/2-inch thick circle; cut with biscuit cutter dipped in flour and place dough onto greased baking sheet. Bake in 450-degree oven 12 to 15 minutes.

Makes 12 to 14 biscuits

Cheesy Corn Bread

2	CUPS ALL-PURPOSE FLOUR
1/4	CUP SUGAR
3	TEASPOONS BAKING POWDER
1	TEASPOON SALT
1	EGG, SLIGHTLY BEATEN
1	CUP MILK
1/2	CUP SHREDDED CHEDDAR CHEESE
1	7-OUNCE CAN WHOLE KERNEL CORN, DRAINED
2	TABLESPOONS CHOPPED RED BELL PEPPER
2	TABLESPOONS CHOPPED GREEN ONION
1/4	CUP VEGETABLE OIL

Heat oven to 400 degrees. Grease square baking pan, 8x8x2 or 9x9x2 inches. Combine all ingredients in bowl; stir just until moistened. Batter should be lumpy. Spread evenly in pan. Bake in 8-inch pan for 45 minutes, 9-inch pan for 35 minutes, or until golden brown.

Yields 9 servings

Zucchini Bread

4	CUPS COARSELY SHREDDED ZUCCHINI
3	CUPS ALL-PURPOSE FLOUR
2 1/2	CUPS SUGAR
1 1/4	CUPS VEGETABLE OIL
4	EGGS, BEATEN
1	TABLESPOON PLUS 1 TEASPOON VANILLA
2	TEASPOONS GROUND CINNAMON
1 1/2	TEASPOONS SALT
1 1/2	TEASPOONS BAKING SODA
1	TEASPOON GROUND CLOVES
1/2	TEASPOON BAKING POWDER
1	CUP CHOPPED NUTS

Heat oven to 325 degrees. Generously grease bottoms only of two 9x5x3 inch-baking pans. Beat all ingredients on low speed, scraping bowl constantly for 1 minute. Beat on medium speed for 1 minute. Pour into pans. Bake until wooden pick inserted into center comes out clean, about 1 hour. Cool for 10 minutes; remove from pans. Cool completely before slicing.

Yields 2 loaves

Almond Cheese Bread

1	CUP SLICED ALMONDS
1	LOAF (1 POUND) FRENCH BREAD
4	TABLESPOONS BUTTER OR MARGARINE, MELTED
2	CLOVES GARLIC, MINCED
1	GREEN PEPPER, THINLY SLICED
1	RED BELL PEPPER, THINLY SLICED
2	CUPS SHREDDED JARLSBERG CHEESE
1/4	CUP SLICED GREEN ONIONS

Spread almonds in shallow pan. Toast at 350 degrees for 10 minutes or until golden, stirring once or twice; cool. Slice bread in half lengthwise. Spread cut surface with mixture of butter and garlic. Arrange pepper rings on top. Combine cheese, almonds and green onions. Sprinkle down center of loaves.

Place on broiling pan; broil 3 inches from heat until cheese melts, about 3 to 5 minutes. Slice to serve. Serve immediately.

Yields 6 servings

Eggnog Muffins

2	CUPS ALL-PURPOSE FLOUR
2/3	CUP SUGAR
1	TABLESPOON BAKING POWDER
1/2	TEASPOON SALT
3/4	CUP EGGNOG
1/2	CUP DARK RUM
5	TABLESPOONS BUTTER OR MARGARINE, MELTED
1	EGG, BEATEN
1/8	TEASPOON GROUND NUTMEG

Heat oven to 400 degrees. Grease bottoms only of 12 medium muffin cups, 2½x1¼ inches, or line with paper baking cups. Sift flour, sugar, baking powder and salt into large bowl. Stir in eggnog, rum, butter, egg and nutmeg, just until flour is moistened (batter will be lumpy). Fill muffin cups about 3/4 full. Bake until golden brown, about 20 minutes. Immediately remove from pan.

Yields 1 dozen muffins

Lemon-Blueberry Pancakes

1 EGG
1 CUP ALL-PURPOSE FLOUR
3/4 CUP MILK
1 TABLESPOON VEGETABLE OIL
3 TEASPOONS BAKING POWDER
1/2 TEASPOON SALT
2 TEASPOONS GRATED LEMON RIND
1 TEASPOON LEMON JUICE
1/2 CUP FRESH OR FROZEN BLUEBERRIES (THAWED AND WELL-DRAINED)

Beat egg with hand beater until fluffy; beat in remaining ingredients except blueberries just until smooth. Fold in blueberries. Grease heated griddle if necessary. (To test griddle, sprinkle with a few drops water. If bubbles skitter around, heat is just right.) For each pancake, pour about 3 tablespoons of batter from tip of large spoon or from pitcher onto hot griddle. Cook pancakes until puffed and dry around edges. Turn and cook other side until golden brown.

Yields about nine 4-inch pancakes

Dilly Cheese Bread

1 PACKAGE ACTIVE DRY YEAST
1/2 CUP WARM WATER (105° TO 115°)
1/2 CUP LUKEWARM MILK (SCALD THEN COOL)
2/3 CUP BUTTER OR MARGARINE, SOFTENED
2 EGGS
1 TEASPOON SALT
3 CUPS ALL-PURPOSE FLOUR
1 CUP SHREDDED CHEDDAR OR SWISS CHEESE (ABOUT 4 OUNCES)
1 TEASPOON DRIED DILLWEED
1/2 TEASPOON PEPPER
 BUTTER OR MARGARINE, SOFTENED

Dissolve yeast in warm water in 2½-quart bowl. Add water, milk, 2/3 cup butter, eggs, salt and 1 cup of flour. Beat on low speed, scraping bowl occasionally, 2 minutes. Stir in remaining flour, cheese, dillweed and pepper. Scrape batter from side of bowl. Cover and let rise in warm place until doubled, about 40 minutes. (Batter is ready if indentation remains when touched with floured hands.)

Stir down batter by beating about 25 strokes. Spread evenly in greased 2-quart casserole. Cover and let rise until doubled, about 45 minutes.

Heat oven to 375 degrees. Place loaf on low rack so that top of casserole is in center of oven. Bake until loaf is brown and sounds hollow when tapped, 40 to 45 minutes. Loosen side of bread from casserole dish; remove immediately. Brush top of bread with softened butter; cool on wire rack.

Yields 1 loaf

Angel Biscuits

2   PACKAGES ACTIVE DRY YEAST
2   TABLESPOONS WARM WATER (105° TO 115°)
1   CUP SHORTENING
5   CUPS SELF-RISING FLOUR
1/4 CUP SUGAR
1   TEASPOON BAKING SODA
2   CUPS BUTTERMILK

Dissolve yeast in warm water. Cut shortening into flour, sugar and baking soda with pastry blender until mixture resembles fine crumbs. Stir in buttermilk and yeast mixture until dough leaves side of bowl (dough will be soft and sticky).

Turn dough onto generously floured, cloth-covered board. Gently roll in flour to coat; shape into ball. Knead 25 to 30 times, sprinkling with flour if dough is too sticky. Place dough in lightly greased bowl; cover and refrigerate at least 3 hours, but no longer than 3 days. Use as needed. Roll or pat dough 1/2 inch thick. Cut with floured 2-inch biscuit cutter. Place about 1 inch apart on greased cookie sheet. Let dough rise in warm place until doubled, about 1 hour.

Heat oven to 400 degrees. Bake until golden brown, 12 to 14 minutes. Immediately remove from cookie sheet.

Yields about 3½ dozen biscuits

Potato Roll Dough

1   PACKAGE ACTIVE DRY YEAST
1 1/2 CUPS WARM WATER (105° TO 115°)
2/3 CUP SUGAR
1 1/2 TEASPOONS SALT
2/3 CUP SHORTENING
2   EGGS, SLIGHTLY BEATEN
1   CUP SLIGHTLY WARM MASHED POTATOES
7 TO 7 1/2 CUPS ALL-PURPOSE FLOUR

Dissolve yeast in warm water. Stir in sugar, salt, shortening, eggs, potatoes and 4 cups of the flour. Beat until smooth. Mix in enough remaining flour to make dough easy to handle.

Turn dough onto lightly floured board; knead until smooth and elastic, about 5 minutes. Place in greased bowl; turn greased-side up. Cover bowl tightly; refrigerate at least 8 hours or until ready to use. (Dough can be kept up to 5 days in refrigerator at 45 degrees or below. Keep covered.)

Punch down dough; divide into 4 parts. Use 1/4 of dough in each of the variations. Let rise 1½ hours before baking. Heat oven to 400 degrees and bake rolls 15 to 25 minutes.

Cloverleafs: Shape bits of dough into 1-inch balls. Place 3 balls in each greased muffin cup. Brush with butter.

Crescents: Roll dough into 12-inch circle, about 1/4 inch thick. Spread with soft butter. Cut into 16 wedges. Roll up, beginning at rounded edge. Place rolls with point underneath on greased baking sheet. Curve slightly. Brush with butter.

Parker House: Roll dough oblong 13x9 inches, about 1/4 inch thick. Cut into 3-inch circles. Brush with butter. Make crease across each circle; fold so top half overlaps slightly. Press edges together in greased 9-inch pan. Brush with butter.

Yields about 3½ to 4 dozens

Basic Sweet Dough

5 1/2 TO 6 CUPS ALL-PURPOSE FLOUR
2   PACKAGES ACTIVE DRY YEAST
3   TABLESPOONS INSTANT NONFAT DRY MILK
1 1/2 TEASPOONS SALT
1/2   CUP SUGAR
1 1/4 CUPS WATER
2/3   CUP BUTTER OR MARGARINE
3   EGGS
1   TEASPOON GRATED LEMON RIND
1   TEASPOON GRATED ORANGE RIND

Combine 3 cups of flour, yeast, dry milk, salt and sugar in large bowl. Heat water and butter over low heat in saucepan until just warm (115 to 120 degrees), stirring constantly. Add to flour mixture; add eggs and grated rind. Beat at low speed for 30 seconds, scraping sides of bowl; beat at high speed for 3 minutes. Stir in 2½ to 3 cups more flour to make a moderately stiff dough. Turn out on lightly floured surface; knead until smooth and elastic, 8 to 10 minutes. Place in greased bowl, turning once to greased surface. (At this time, dough may be tightly covered and refrigerated. When ready to use, punch down and cut off desired portion. Dough can be kept refrigerated four days.) Cover; let rise until doubled. Punch down; cover and let rest 5 minutes before shaping.

CHERRY CANDY CANE COFFEE CAKE

Roll 1/3 of Basic Sweet Dough into rectangle, 15x6 inches. Place on greased baking sheet. Make slits at 1/2-inch intervals. Spread one 16-ounce can cherry pie filling lengthwise down center of rectangle. Crisscross strips over cherries. Stretch rectangle to 22 inches; curve to form cane. Cover; let rise in warm place until doubled, about 1 hour. (Dough is ready if indentation remains when touched.) Heat oven to 350 degrees. Bake until golden brown, 20 to 25 minutes. Drizzle glaze over cane while warm. Decorate with cherry halves or pieces if desired. TO MAKE GLAZE: Blend 1 cup powdered sugar with 1 tablespoon water until smooth.

NOTE: Cinnamon Rolls or other sweet rolls can be made with this dough.

Sweet Potato-Nut Bread

2 1/2 CUPS SUGAR
2/3   CUP VEGETABLE OIL
4   EGGS
1   16-OUNCE CAN SWEET POTATOES OR YAMS, DRAINED
2/3   CUP WATER
3 1/3 CUPS ALL-PURPOSE FLOUR
2   TEASPOONS BAKING SODA
1 1/2 TEASPOONS SALT
1   TEASPOON GROUND CINNAMON
1   TEASPOON GROUND CLOVES
1/2   TEASPOON BAKING POWDER
1   CUP CHOPPED NUTS

Heat oven to 350 degrees. Grease bottoms only of two 9x5x3-inch loaf pans. Mix sugar, oil, eggs, sweet potatoes and water in large bowl. Stir in remaining ingredients. Pour into pans. Bake until wooden pick inserted in center comes out clean, about 1 hour 10 minutes; cool slightly. Loosen sides of loaves from pans; remove from pans. Cool completely before slicing. To store, wrap and refrigerate no longer than 10 days.

Yields 2 loaves

Sweet Potato Pancakes

2 CUPS BUTTERMILK BISCUIT MIX
2 TABLESPOONS LIGHT BROWN SUGAR
1 TEASPOON GROUND CINNAMON
1/2 TEASPOON GROUND NUTMEG
1 1/2 CUPS EVAPORATED MILK
1/2 CUP COOKED MASHED SWEET POTATOES
2 TABLESPOONS VEGETABLE OIL
2 EGGS, SLIGHTLY BEATEN
1 TEASPOON VANILLA
1/2 TEASPOON GRATED ORANGE RIND

Combine biscuit mix, sugar, cinnamon and nutmeg in large mixer bowl. Add milk, sweet potatoes, oil, eggs, vanilla and rind; beat until smooth. Grease heated griddle if necessary. For each pancake pour about 3 tablespoons batter from tip of large spoon or from pitcher onto hot griddle. Cook until top surface is bubbly and edges are dry. Turn; cook until golden brown. Keep pancakes warm. Serve with syrup.

Yields 12 to 16 pancakes

Pecan Pancakes

1 EGG
1 CUP ALL-PURPOSE FLOUR
1 TABLESPOON BAKING POWDER
1 TABLESPOON SUGAR
1/4 TEASPOON SALT
3/4 CUP MILK
1 TABLESPOON VEGETABLE OIL
1/2 CUP CHOPPED PECANS

Beat egg with hand beater until fluffy; beat in remaining ingredients except pecans until just smooth. Grease heated griddle if necessary. For each pancake, pour about 3 tablespoons batter from tip of large spoon or from pitcher onto hot griddle. When pancakes begin to cook (bubbles will appear), sprinkle a few chopped pecans over each pancake. Turn and cook other side until golden brown.

Yields about nine 4-inch pancakes

Rolled Cheese Biscuits

2 CUPS ALL-PURPOSE FLOUR
1 TABLESPOON SUGAR
3 TEASPOONS BAKING POWDER
1 TEASPOON SALT
1/2 CUP VEGETABLE SHORTENING
3/4 CUP MILK
1 CUP GRATED CHEDDAR CHEESE
   PAPRIKA

Heat oven to 350. Sift flour, sugar, baking powder and salt. Cut shortening into flour mixture with pastry blender until mixture resembles fine crumbs. Stir in milk until dough leaves side of bowl. (Dough will be soft and sticky.) Turn dough onto lightly floured surface. Knead lightly 10 times. Flatten dough with hands or rolling pin into rectangle, 12x7 inches. Sprinkle with cheese and paprika; roll up tightly, beginning at 12-inch side. Pinch edges of dough into roll to seal well. Stretch roll to make even. Cut into 10 to 12 one-inch slices. Place slightly apart in greased 8x1½-inch round pan. Bake for 10 to 15 minutes.

Makes about 1 dozen biscuits

Jet Rolls (No Knead)

2   PACKAGES ACTIVE DRY YEAST
1   CUP WARM WATER (105° TO 115°)
1 1/3   CUPS MILK
2/3   CUP BUTTER OR MARGARINE
3/4   CUP SUGAR
1/2   TEASPOON SALT
2   EGGS, BEATEN
6 1/2 TO 7 CUPS FLOUR
SOFTENED BUTTER OR MARGARINE

Dissolve yeast in warm water. Heat milk until warm. Pour into large bowl. Add butter; stirring until butter melts. Stir in yeast mixture, sugar, salt and eggs. Slowly stir in flour, mixing until soft dough is formed.

Cover; let rise in warm place until doubled, about 1 hour. (Dough will be sticky.) Turn dough onto heavily floured board; roll to form ball. Divide dough into thirds; roll each third 1/2-inch thick, with floured 2 ¾-inch round cutter; cut circles. Repeat with remaining dough. Melt 1/2 cup butter in small saucepan; dip both sides of each circle in butter and fold in half. Arrange closely in pie pans. Cover; let rolls rise until doubled, about 45 minutes.

Heat oven to 350 degrees. Bake 15 to 20 minutes or until golden brown.

Yields about 4 dozen

Easy Corn Muffins

1   CUP YELLOW CORNMEAL
1   CUP ALL-PURPOSE FLOUR
1   TABLESPOON BAKING POWDER
1   TABLESPOON SUGAR
1/2   TEASPOON SALT
1   CUP BUTTERMILK
1   EGG, SLIGHTLY BEATEN
1/4   CUP VEGETABLE OIL

Heat oven to 425 degrees. Grease bottoms only of 12 medium muffin cups or line with paper baking cups. Combine cornmeal, flour, baking powder, sugar and salt. Stir in milk, egg and vegetable oil. Mix until just moistened. Fill muffin cups about 3/4 full. Bake for 20 to 25 minutes. Immediately remove from pan.

Yields 12 muffins

Easy Corn Muffins

Golden Apple Bran Muffins

2	LARGE GOLDEN DELICIOUS APPLES, PARED, CORED AND CHOPPED (ABOUT 2 1/2 CUPS)
1/2	CUP BUTTER OR MARGARINE
1	CUP BOILING WATER
3	CUPS WHOLE BRAN CEREAL
2	CUPS BUTTERMILK
2	EGGS, SLIGHTLY BEATEN
2/3	CUP SUGAR
1	CUP RAISINS
2 1/2	CUPS ALL-PURPOSE FLOUR
2 1/2	TEASPOONS BAKING SODA
2	TEASPOONS GROUND CINNAMON
1	TEASPOON GROUND NUTMEG
1/2	TEASPOON GROUND CLOVES
1/2	TEASPOON SALT

Cook apples in butter until tender, about 10 minutes. Pour boiling water over bran; add apples, buttermilk, eggs, sugar and raisins. Combine flour, baking soda, spices and salt; stir into bran mixture just until combined. Refrigerate in tightly covered container at least 24 hours. For optimum quality use within two weeks. Fill greased muffin pans 3/4 full and bake at 400 degrees, 20 to 25 minutes or until wooden pick inserted near center comes out clean.

Yields about 30 muffins

DESSERTS
▼▼▼▼▼▼▼▼▼▼▼▼▼▼▼▼▼▼

Summer Fruit Pie

Summer Fruit Pie

PASTRY FOR 9-INCH, ONE-CRUST PIE

1   8-OUNCE PACKAGE CREAM CHEESE, SOFTENED

1/4   CUP SIFTED POWDERED SUGAR

2 TO 3 TABLESPOONS ORANGE LIQUEUR

2   TEASPOONS GRATED ORANGE PEEL

6   CUPS MIXED FRESH FRUIT SUCH AS STRAWBERRIES, RASPBERRIES, SLICED BANANAS, SLICED PITTED PLUMS, BLUEBERRIES, PINEAPPLE SLICES OR PEACHES

1   8-OUNCE JAR CURRANT JELLY

3   TABLESPOONS ORANGE LIQUEUR

SUGAR

Heat oven to 475 degrees. Place pastry in pie plate, pressing firmly against bottom and side. Decorate edges of pie crust. Prick bottom and side thoroughly with fork. Bake until light brown, 8 to 10 minutes; cool. Mix cream cheese, powdered sugar, 2 to 3 tablespoons orange liqueur and orange peel until smooth. Fill pie shell. Arrange mixed fresh fruit over filling. Melt currant jelly and 3 tablespoons of orange liqueur in small saucepan; cool slightly. Brush on top of mixed fruit with pastry brush. Chill. Garnish with sugar and mint leaves if desired.

Yields 1 pie

Lemon Meringue Pie

1 1/2 CUPS SUGAR

1/4   CUP PLUS 2 TABLESPOONS CORNSTARCH

1/4   TEASPOON SALT

1/2   CUP COLD WATER

1/2   CUP FRESH LEMON JUICE

3   EGG YOLKS, WELL-BEATEN

2   TABLESPOONS BUTTER OR MARGARINE

1 1/2 CUPS BOILING WATER

GRATED PEEL OF LEMON

1   9-INCH BAKED PIE CRUST

MERINGUE

4   EGG WHITES

1/4   TEASPOON CREAM OF TARTAR

CUP SUGAR

Combine the sugar, cornstarch, and salt thoroughly. Gradually blend in cold water and lemon juice. Stir in the egg yolks. Add the butter and boiling water. Bring to a boil and boil for 1 minute. Remove from heat and stir in lemon peel. Pour into baked pie crust. Top with Meringue, sealing edges well. Bake at 350 degrees for 12 to 15 minutes, or until lightly browned. Cool for 2 hours before serving. To make Meringue, beat with an electric mixer the egg whites with the cream of tartar until foamy in a bowl. Gradually add the sugar and beat until stiff peaks form.

Yields 1 pie

Walnut Sweet Potato Pie

1   9-INCH PASTRY SHELL

1   POUND SWEET POTATOES OR YAMS, COOKED AND PEELED (ABOUT 2 MEDIUM)

1/4   CUP BUTTER OR MARGARINE

1   14-OUNCE CAN SWEETENED CONDENSED MILK

1   TEASPOON GRATED ORANGE RIND

1   TEASPOON VANILLA

1   TEASPOON GROUND CINNAMON

1/2	TEASPOON GROUND NUTMEG
1/4	TEASPOON SALT
2	EGGS, SLIGHTLY BEATEN
	WALNUT TOPPING

Heat oven to 350 degrees. Beat hot yams with butter until smooth in large mixer bowl. Add remaining ingredients except pastry shell and Walnut Topping, setting aside pastry shell and Walnut Topping; mix until creamy consistency. Pour into pastry shell. Bake 30 minutes. Remove pie from oven; spoon Walnut Topping evenly over top. Bake 20 to 25 minutes longer or until pie is golden brown. Cool. Serve warm or chilled. Refrigerate leftovers.

WALNUT TOPPING: Combine 1 egg, 3 tablespoons dark corn syrup, 3 tablespoons firmly packed light brown sugar, 1 tablespoon melted butter or margarine and 1/2 teaspoon maple flavoring in small bowl; mix well. Stir in 1 cup chopped walnuts.

Yields 1 pie

Buttermilk Pie With Mixed Berry Compote

	PASTRY FOR 9-INCH PIE
4	EGGS
3/4	CUP SUGAR
2	TABLESPOONS ALL-PURPOSE FLOUR
4	TABLESPOONS MELTED BUTTER OR MARGARINE
1	TEASPOON VANILLA
1/4	TEASPOON SALT
3/4	CUP BUTTERMILK
	GROUND NUTMEG

Heat oven to 350 degrees. Prepare pastry. Line pie plate with pastry. Beat eggs; add sugar, flour, butter, vanilla and salt. Mix thoroughly; blend in buttermilk. Pour into pastry-lined pie plate. Sprinkle lightly with nutmeg. Bake for 40 to 50 minutes or until toothpick inserted in center comes out clean. Serve with Mixed Berry Compote if desired.

MIXED BERRY COMPOTE

1	10-OUNCE PACKAGE FROZEN RED RASPBERRIES, THAWED
2	TABLESPOONS CORNSTARCH
2	TABLESPOONS SUGAR
1	CUP SLICED FRESH STRAWBERRIES
1/2	CUP FRESH OR FROZEN BLACKBERRIES
1/2	CUP FRESH OR FROZEN BLUEBERRIES
1	TEASPOON GRATED ORANGE RIND

Drain raspberries, reserving syrup. Combine cornstarch and sugar in small saucepan. Stir in reserved syrup and cook over medium heat until sauce thickens; cool. Stir in remaining ingredients. Serve over buttermilk pie slices.

Yields 1 pie

Sweet Potato Cake

1	CUP BUTTER OR MARGARINE, SOFTENED
2	CUPS SUGAR
2 1/2	CUPS MASHED COOKED SWEET POTATOES
4	EGGS
3	CUPS SIFTED ALL-PURPOSE FLOUR
1/4	TEASPOON SALT
2	TEASPOONS BAKING POWDER
1	TEASPOON BAKING SODA
1	TEASPOON GROUND CINNAMON
1/2	TEASPOON GROUND NUTMEG
1	TEASPOON VANILLA EXTRACT
1	TEASPOON ORANGE EXTRACT

Thoroughly cream butter and sugar; add sweet potatoes and beat until light and fluffy. Add eggs, one at a time, beating well after each addition. Sift together flour, salt, baking powder, baking soda, cinnamon, nutmeg; gradually add to creamed mixture, beating well after each addition. Blend in vanilla and orange extracts. Pour into a greased and floured 10-inch tube pan. Bake in 350-degree oven for 1 hour and 15 minutes, or until done. Cool about 5 minutes and remove from pan. While still hot drizzle with glaze.

GLAZE

Combine 1 cup sifted powdered sugar, 4½ teaspoons fresh orange juice, 1/2 teaspoon grated lemon rind and 1/2 teaspoon grated orange rind and mix well.

Yields 1 ten-inch cake

Greenie's Sweet Potato Pie

	PASTRY FOR 9-INCH, ONE-CRUST PIE
3/4	CUP SUGAR
1	TABLESPOON ALL-PURPOSE FLOUR
1/2	TEASPOON BAKING POWDER
1/2	TEASPOON GROUND NUTMEG
2	CUPS COOKED MASHED SWEET POTATOES (ABOUT 2 MEDIUM POTATOES)
1/4	CUP BUTTER OR MARGARINE
1	EGG, SLIGHTLY BEATEN
1	TABLESPOON LEMON JUICE
1	TEASPOON VANILLA EXTRACT
1 1/4	CUPS MILK OR EVAPORATED MILK

Heat oven to 425 degrees. Prepare pastry. Combine sugar, flour, baking powder and nutmeg in medium mixing bowl; add remaining ingredients and beat until blended well. Place pastry-lined pie plate on oven rack; pour in filling. Bake 15 minutes. Reduce oven to 350 degrees. Bake until knife inserted in center comes out clean, about 45 minutes longer.

Yields 1 pie

Old-Fashioned Apple Pie

	PASTRY FOR 9-INCH, TWO-CRUST PIE
1/2	CUP SUGAR
1/4	CUP PACKED BROWN SUGAR
1/4	CUP ALL-PURPOSE FLOUR
2	TEASPOONS FRESH LEMON JUICE
1/2	TEASPOON GROUND CINNAMON

1/2 TEASPOON GROUND NUTMEG

DASH SALT

6 TO 7 CUPS THINLY SLICED, PARED, TART APPLES (ABOUT 6 MEDIUM)

2 TABLESPOONS BUTTER OR MARGARINE

Heat oven to 425 degrees. Prepare pastry. Line pie plate with one pastry crust. Mix sugars, flour, lemon juice, cinnamon, nutmeg and salt. Toss apples with sugar mixture. Pour into pastry-lined pie plate. Dot with butter. Cover with top crust that has slits cut in it; seal by moistening rim of bottom crust. Fold edge under bottom crust, pressing to seal. Make a decorative edge. Cover edge with 3-inch strips of aluminum foil during last 15 minutes of bake time. Bake until crust is light brown and juice begins to bubble through slits in crust, 40 to 50 minutes.

Yields 1 pie

Old-Fashioned Baked Rice Pudding

4 EGGS, BEATEN

3 CUPS MILK

1/3 CUP SUGAR

1/4 TEASPOON SALT (OPTIONAL)

2 TEASPOONS VANILLA

2 TEASPOONS GRATED LEMON RIND

2 CUPS COOKED RICE

GROUND NUTMEG

Combine all ingredients except nutmeg and pour into a 2½-quart baking dish. Set dish in pan of hot water. Bake at 300 for 1 hour; after 30 minutes insert spoon at edge of pudding and stir from bottom. Continue to bake until knife inserted near center of pudding comes out clean. Sprinkle with ground nutmeg. Serve hot or cold.

RAISIN RICE PUDDING: Prepare rice pudding as directed above. Add 1/2 cup seedless raisins to mixture before baking. Spread cooled baked pudding with 2 cups whipped cream and sprinkle with a mixture of 2 teaspoons sugar and 1 teaspoon ground cinnamon. Brown quickly under broiler.

Yields 6 to 8 servings

Citrus Ambrosia

2 EGGS

1/2 CUP SUGAR

GRATED PEEL OF 1/2 LEMON

1/4 CUP FRESH SQUEEZED LEMON JUICE

1/4 CUP BUTTER OR MARGARINE

2 ORANGES, PEELED AND CUT INTO HALF-CARTWHEEL SLICES

1 GRAPEFRUIT, PEELED AND SECTIONED

2 TANGERINES, PEELED, SEGMENTED AND SEEDED

TOASTED SHREDDED OR FLAKED COCONUT

CHERRIES

MINT LEAVES

To make the sauce, in a saucepan, beat the eggs well. Stir in the sugar, lemon peel, lemon juice and butter. Cook over low heat, stirring constantly, until thickened, about 10 minutes. Cover and chill.

Divide fruit into 4 individual dessert dishes or shallow champagne glasses and chill. Spoon the sauce over the fruit, sprinkle with coconut and garnish with cherries and mint.

Yields 4 servings

Old-Fashioned Caramel Cake

1	CUP SOUR CREAM
1/4	CUP MILK
2/3	CUP BUTTER OR MARGARINE
1 3/4	CUPS SUGAR
2	EGGS
1	TEASPOON VANILLA
1	TEASPOON ALMOND EXTRACT
2 3/4	CUPS ALL-PURPOSE FLOUR
2 1/2	TEASPOONS BAKING POWDER
1	TEASPOON SALT

Combine sour cream and milk; set aside. Heat oven to 350 degrees. Grease and flour 2 round 9x1½-inch pans. Mix butter, sugar, eggs, vanilla and almond extract in large mixer bowl until fluffy. Beat on high speed, scraping bowl occasionally, for 5 minutes. Combine flour, baking powder and salt; add to creamed mixture alternately with sour cream mixture, beginning and ending with dry flour mixture. Pour batter into prepared pans.

Bake until wooden pick inserted in center comes out clean, 30 to 35 minutes. Cool layers for 10 minutes; remove from pans and cool completely. Fill and frost layers with Caramel Frosting.

CARAMEL FROSTING

3	CUPS SUGAR, DIVIDED
1	TABLESPOON ALL-PURPOSE FLOUR
1	CUP MILK
3/4	CUP BUTTER OR MARGARINE
1	TEASPOON VANILLA

Sprinkle 1/2 cup sugar in shallow, heavy 3½-quart Dutch oven; place over medium heat. Cook, stirring constantly, until sugar dissolves and syrup is light golden brown. Remove from heat.

Combine remaining 2½ cups sugar and flour, stirring well; add milk and bring to a boil, stirring constantly. Gradually pour 1/4 hot mixture into caramelized sugar, stirring constantly; add remaining hot mixture (mixture will lump), but continue to stir until smooth.

Return to hot. Cover mixture; cook over low heat for 2 minutes. Uncover and cook (uncovered) over medium heat until candy thermometer reaches 238. Add butter, stirring to blend. Remove from heat and cool without stirring until temperature drops to 110 (about 1 hour). Add vanilla and beat with wooden spoon or with an electric hand mixer until it is of spreading consistency.

Yields 1 cake

Chocolate Sheet Cake With Fudge Frosting

2	CUPS SUGAR
2	CUPS SIFTED ALL-PURPOSE FLOUR
1	TEASPOON BAKING SODA
1/2	TEASPOON SALT
1/2	CUP BUTTER OR MARGARINE
1	CUP WATER
1/4	CUP COCOA
1/2	CUP BUTTERMILK
2	EGGS, BEATEN
1	TEASPOON VANILLA

Heat oven to 400 degrees. Sift together sugar, flour, baking soda and salt. Combine butter, water and cocoa in saucepan; stirring constantly, bring to rolling boil over medium heat. Add to dry ingredients, mixing well. Stir in buttermilk, eggs and vanilla. Turn into greased 15x10x1-inch baking pan. Bake for 20 minutes or until done. Frost in pan, warm or cooled.

FUDGE FROSTING

1 1/2	CUPS SUGAR
6	TABLESPOONS MARGARINE
6	TABLESPOONS MILK
1	TABLESPOON LIGHT CORN SYRUP
2/3	CUP SEMISWEET CHOCOLATE PIECES
2/3	CUP CHOPPED NUTS

Combine first 4 ingredients in 2-quart saucepan. Stirring constantly, bring to a rolling boil over medium heat; boil 3 minutes. Turn off heat. Add chocolate pieces; stir until chocolate is melted and frosting starts to thicken. Pour over cake, spreading quickly to cover. Nuts may be stirred into frosting or sprinkled on top of frosted cake.

Yields 1 cake

Apple Dumplings

	PASTRY FOR 9-INCH, TWO-CRUST PIE
6	BAKING APPLES (EACH ABOUT 3 INCHES IN DIAMETER), PARED AND CORED
1/4	CUP RAISINS
1/4	CUP CHOPPED WALNUTS
1/2	TEASPOON GROUND CINNAMON
2 1/2	CUPS PACKED BROWN SUGAR
1 1/2	CUPS WATER

Heat oven to 425 degrees. Prepare pastry. Gather into ball. Roll 2/3 of pastry into 14-inch square on lightly floured board; cut into four squares. Roll remaining pastry into rectangle, 14x7 inches; cut into two squares. Place apple on each square.

Mix raisins, nuts and cinnamon; fill each apple. Moisten corners of each pastry square; bring two opposite corners up over apple and pinch together. Repeat with remaining corners; pinch edges of pastry to seal. Place dumplings in ungreased 13x9x2-inch baking dish.

Heat brown sugar and water to boiling; carefully pour around dumplings. Bake, spooning or basting syrup over dumplings two or three times, until crust is golden and apples are tender, about 40 minutes. Serve warm or cool with ice cream or sweetened whipped cream if desired.

Yields 6 servings

Apple Dumplings

Lemonade Cake

1	18½-OUNCE PACKAGE LEMON CAKE MIX
1	3⅛-OUNCE PACKAGE LEMON INSTANT PUDDING AND PIE FILLING
4	EGGS
1	CUP WATER
1/4	CUP VEGETABLE OIL
1	6-OUNCE CAN FROZEN LEMONADE, THAWED
2	CUPS SIFTED POWDERED SUGAR

Combine cake mix, pudding mix, eggs, water and oil; blend well, then beat 4 minutes at medium speed. Turn into greased and floured 13x9x2-inch baking pan. Bake in 350-degree oven for 45 to 50 minutes or until done. Cool in pan 5 minutes, then prick cake with 2-tined fork or skewer completely through to bottom of cake. Thoroughly blend lemonade concentrate and powdered sugar. Gradually spoon glaze over cake until completely absorbed. Cool and cut into squares.

Yields 1 cake

Easy Pineapple Upside-Down Cake

1/2	CUP BUTTER OR MARGARINE
1	CUP PACKED BROWN SUGAR
1	16-OUNCE CAN PINEAPPLE SLICES, DRAINED
	MARASCHINO CHERRIES
1	18 ½-OUNCE PACKAGE YELLOW CAKE MIX
1	TEASPOON GRATED ORANGE RIND

Divide butter and brown sugar evenly in half. Place half of the butter into two 9-inch round cake pans. Melt butter over low heat. Sprinkle half of the brown sugar evenly over butter in both pans. Arrange pineapple slices over sugar in each pan. Garnish with cherries. Prepare cake mix as directed on package and stir in rind. Pour half of the batter evenly over fruit in each pan. Bake in 350-degree oven for 35 to 45 minutes or until done. Invert at once on serving plate. Leave pan over cake a few minutes. Serve warm.

Yields 2 nine-inch cakes

Blueberry-Peach Cobbler

1	PASTRY FOR 10-INCH PIE CRUST
1/2	CUP SUGAR
2	TABLESPOONS ALL-PURPOSE FLOUR
5	CUPS SLICED, FRESH OR FROZEN PEACHES
1/4	TEASPOON GROUND NUTMEG
1/2	TEASPOON VANILLA EXTRACT
1	CUP FRESH OR FROZEN BLUEBERRIES
1	TABLESPOON BUTTER OR MARGARINE, CUT INTO SMALL PIECES
	SUGAR

Heat oven to 400 degrees. Roll pastry to fit a 9x9-inch baking dish. Combine sugar and flour. Gently mix peaches, sugar mixture, nutmeg and vanilla. Gently fold in blueberries and butter. Pour peach mixture into 9x9-inch baking dish. Cover with the crust that has slits cut into it; seal and flute. If desired, sprinkle with sugar. Bake until crust is brown and juice begins to bubble through slits in crust, about 40 to 50 minutes.

Yields 6 servings

Brown Sugar Pound Cake

1/2	CUP BUTTER OR MARGARINE
1	CUP SHORTENING
1	CUP SUGAR
2	CUPS FIRMLY PACKED LIGHT BROWN SUGAR
2	TEASPOONS VANILLA
6	EGGS
3 1/3	CUPS SIFTED CAKE FLOUR
1/2	TEASPOON BAKING POWDER
1/2	TEASPOON SALT
1	CUP EVAPORATED MILK
1	CUP FLAKED COCONUT
1	CUP CHOPPED NUTS

Cream butter and shortening; gradually add sugar and brown sugar, beating until light and fluffy. Blend in vanilla. Add eggs, one at a time, beating well after each addition. Sift together flour, baking powder and salt; add to creamed mixture alternately with evaporated milk, mixing well. Fold in coconut and nuts. Pour into well-greased and floured 10-inch tube pan. Bake in 325-degree oven for 1 hour and 40 minutes or until done.

GLAZE

1/3	CUP BUTTER OR MARGARINE
1	CUP FIRMLY PACKED LIGHT BROWN SUGAR
1/4	CUP EVAPORATED MILK
1	TEASPOON VANILLA

Melt butter over medium heat in saucepan; blend in sugar. Add milk and bring to a rolling boil; boil for 2 minutes. Turn off heat; cool. Add vanilla and beat until it is of spreading consistency.

Easy Fruit Pizza

1	1-POUND 4-OUNCE PACKAGE REFRIGERATED SUGAR COOKIE DOUGH

GLAZE

1/4	CUP SUGAR
1	TABLESPOON CORNSTARCH
3/4	CUP FRESH ORANGE JUICE

CHEESE FILLING

1	8-OUNCE PACKAGE CREAM CHEESE, SOFTENED
1/3	CUP SUGAR
2	TABLESPOONS SOUR CREAM
1/2	TEASPOON GRATED LEMON RIND
1/2	TEASPOON VANILLA EXTRACT

TOPPING

STRAWBERRIES, SLICED PEACHES, BLUEBERRIES, GRAPES OR YOUR CHOICE OF FRUIT

Heat oven to 400 degrees. Press cookie dough onto 12-inch round pizza pan. Bake until light brown, 10 to 13 minutes. Cool.

Meanwhile, prepare glaze. Combine sugar and cornstarch; blend well in 1-quart saucepan. Add juice; cook over medium heat, stirring constantly, until mixture comes to boil. Boil 1 to 2 minutes. Cool 10 minutes.

Beat together filling ingredients until smooth with electric mixer. Spoon filling onto cool pie crust.

Arrange fruit on cheese mixture. Drizzle glaze over fruit. Cut into wedges to serve.

Yields 8 servings

Bourbon Pecan Cake

1	POUND SEEDLESS GOLDEN RAISINS
1	CUP BOURBON
1	CUP BUTTER, SOFTENED
2	CUPS SUGAR
6	EGGS
3 1/2	CUPS SIFTED ALL-PURPOSE FLOUR
2	TEASPOONS BAKING POWDER
1	TEASPOON SALT
1	POUND COARSELY CHOPPED PECANS

Soak raisins in bourbon overnight. Cream butter and sugar. Gradually add eggs, one at a time, beating after each addition. Sift together flour, baking powder and salt; add flour mixture. Add soaked raisins and pecans, mixing well. Pour batter into greased and floured tube or bundt pan. Bake at 325 degrees for 1½ hours or until cake is done. Cool cake on rack. After cooling, wrap in cloth towel that has been soaked with bourbon and place in airtight container.

Yields 1 cake

Sour Cream Pound Cake

1 1/2	CUPS BUTTER OR MARGARINE
3	CUPS SUGAR
6	EGGS
1 1/2	TEASPOONS VANILLA EXTRACT
1 1/2	TEASPOONS RUM EXTRACT
3	CUPS CAKE FLOUR
1/2	TEASPOON SALT
1	CUP SOUR CREAM

1/4	TEASPOON BAKING SODA

Cream butter; gradually add sugar, beating until light and fluffy. Add eggs, one at a time, beating well after each addition; blend in vanilla and rum extract. Sift flour with salt; add alternately with sour cream, reserving 2 tablespoons sour cream. Blend baking soda into reserved sour cream and add to batter, stirring to blend. Pour into greased and floured 10-inch tube pan. Bake in 325-degree oven for 1½ hours or until done.

Yields 1 cake

Bread Pudding with Whiskey Sauce

2	CUPS MILK
1/4	CUP BUTTER OR MARGARINE, MELTED
2	EGGS, SLIGHTLY BEATEN
3/4	CUP SUGAR
1	TEASPOON GROUND CINNAMON
1/4	TEASPOON GROUND NUTMEG
1	TEASPOON VANILLA EXTRACT
1/4	TEASPOON SALT
6	CUPS CUBED FRENCH BREAD
1/2	CUP RAISINS

Heat oven to 350 degrees. Combine milk, butter, eggs, sugar, cinnamon, nutmeg, vanilla and salt in large bowl. Stir in bread cubes and raisins; pour bread mixture into 1½ quart ungreased casserole. Place casserole in pan of very hot water, about 1 inch deep.

Bake uncovered until knife inserted in center comes out clean, about 40 to 45 minutes. Serve warm with Whiskey Sauce.

WHISKEY SAUCE

1/2 CUP BUTTER OR MARGARINE
1 EGG
1 CUP SUGAR
1/4 CUP WHISKEY

Cook and stir sugar and butter in heavy saucepan until mixture is very hot and sugar is dissolved. Add small amount of sugar mixture to egg and stir together. Add egg quickly and beat together until smooth. Cool slightly and add whiskey. Serve over pudding.

Yields 8 servings

Summer Berry Tart

CRUST:

1   9-INCH REFRIGERATED READY PIE CRUST AT ROOM TEMPERATURE
1   TABLESPOON ALL-PURPOSE FLOUR

FILLING:

1   8-OUNCE PACKAGE CREAM CHEESE, SOFTENED
1/4   CUP SIFTED POWDERED SUGAR
1   TEASPOON GRATED LIME RIND
2   TABLESPOONS WHIPPING CREAM
1   PINT FRESH STRAWBERRIES
1/2   PINT FRESH BLACKBERRIES
1/2   PINT FRESH RASPBERRIES
1/2   CUP FRESH BLUEBERRIES

GLAZE:

1   8-OUNCE JAR CURRANT JELLY
2   TABLESPOONS KIRSCH (CLEAR CHERRY BRANDY OR ORANGE JUICE)

Heat oven to 400 degrees. Unfold crust and press out fold lines. Sprinkle with flour and gently spread flour over crust. Arrange flour-side down in 9-inch tart pan with removable bottom. Trim edges. Pierce all over with fork. Bake until golden brown, about 15 minutes. Cool on rack.

Mix cream cheese, powdered sugar, lime rind and whipping cream until smooth. Spread cream cheese mixture in tart shell. Arrange berries on top.

Melt currant jelly and kirsch in small saucepan; cook slightly. Brush on top of berries with pastry brush. Serve.

Yields 1 tart

Double-Dipped Strawberries

8 TO 10 LARGE STRAWBERRIES WITH LEAVES INTACT
2   2-OUNCE PACKAGES WHITE CHOCOLATE CANDY COATING
1   6-OUNCE PACKAGE SEMISWEET CHOCOLATE CHIPS

Melt the white chocolate coating in small saucepan over low heat, stirring constantly. Remove from heat. Holding a strawberry by its green cap, dip a portion of the strawberry into melted coating. Let excess coating drop off strawberry. Place on a baking sheet lined with wax paper and let dry. Repeat with remaining strawberries.

In another small saucepan, melt chocolate over low heat, stirring constantly. Dip strawberry in melted chocolate, leaving part of the white coating showing. Let excess coating drop off berry. Let dry, then chill.

Yields 4 to 6 servings

Peach Fried Pies

2   6-OUNCE PACKAGES DRIED PEACHES
1/2   CUP SUGAR
2   TABLESPOONS FRESH LEMON JUICE
1/2   TEASPOON GROUND CINNAMON
1/2   TEASPOON GROUND NUTMEG
     EGG PASTRY
     VEGETABLE OIL

Cook peaches according to package directions; drain and mash. Combine with sugar, lemon juice and spices. Roll out pastry; cut into 5-inch rounds. Place 3 tablespoons peach filling on half of round. Moisten edges with water; fold in half, pressing edges together with fork to seal. In skillet, fry pies in 1 inch of hot oil (375 degrees) until golden brown on each side, turning only once. Drain well on paper towels.

EGG PASTRY

3   CUPS ALL-PURPOSE FLOUR
1   TEASPOON SALT
1   CUP SHORTENING
1   EGG, BEATEN
4   TABLESPOONS COLD WATER
1   TEASPOON VINEGAR

Combine flour and salt; cut in shortening until mixture resembles coarse cornmeal. Combine egg, water and vinegar; sprinkle over flour mixture, stirring lightly to form a ball. Wrap in wax paper; chill at least 1 hour or until ready to use.

NOTE: Dried apples or 2 cups cooked mashed sweet potatoes can be substituted for peaches.

Yields about 1½ dozen

Oatmeal Raisin Cookies

1   CUP BUTTER OR MARGARINE, SOFTENED
3/4   CUP PACKED BROWN SUGAR
3/4   CUP SUGAR
2   EGGS
1   TEASPOON VANILLA
1 1/2 CUPS ALL-PURPOSE FLOUR
1   TEASPOON BAKING SODA
1   TEASPOON GROUND CINNAMON
1/2   TEASPOON SALT
3   CUPS OATS, UNCOOKED (QUICK OR OLD-FASHIONED)
1   CUP RAISINS

Heat oven to 350 degrees. Beat butter, brown sugar and sugar until creamy. Add eggs and vanilla; beat well. Combine flour, baking soda, cinnamon and salt; add to butter mixture, mixing well. Stir in oats and raisins; mix well. Drop by rounded tablespoonfuls onto ungreased cookie sheet. Bake 10 to 12 minutes or until light golden brown. Cool 1 minute on cookie sheet; remove to wire rack. Cool completely.

Yields about 4 dozen

TIMELY TIPS

▼ ▼

SIMPLE SUBSTITUTIONS

Recipe Calls For	Substitute
Baking Powder	2 parts cream of tartar to 1 part baking soda for a single-acting baking powder
Beef Broth or Stock	1 beef bouillon cube dissolved in 1 cup boiling water
Bread Crumbs	3/4 cup cracker crumbs for each cup
Brown Sugar	1 to 2 tablespoons molasses to 1 cup of granulated sugar
Butter	1 cup margarine or 7/8 cup vegetable oil, lard, or vegetable shortening for 1 cup butter
Buttermilk	1 tablespoon lemon juice or white vinegar added to 1 cup milk (let stand for about 10 minutes) or use 1 cup plain low-fat yogurt
Chicken Broth or Stock	1 chicken bouillon cube dissolved in 1 cup boiling water
Chocolate	3 tablespoons cocoa powder plus 1 tablespoon unsalted butter for 1 ounce of unsweetened chocolate or use 3 tablespoons carob powder plus 2 tablespoons water
Coconut, grated	1⅓ cups flaked coconut
Coconut Milk	3 tablespoons canned cream of coconut plus enough hot water or low-fat milk to equal 1 cup
Cornstarch	2 tablespoons all-purpose flour or 2 teaspoons arrowroot for 1 tablespoon cornstarch
Corn Syrup (dark)	3/4 cup light corn syrup plus 1/4 cup light molasses

▼ ▼ ▼ ▼ ▼ ▼ ▼ ▼ ▼ ▼ ▼ ▼ ▼ ▼ ▼ ▼

Recipe Calls For:	Substitute
Corn Syrup (light)	1¼ cups granulated or packed brown sugar (or dark brown sugar) plus 1/4 cup of the liquid that is required for the recipe
Cream, light	3 tablespoons butter plus enough whole milk to equal 1 cup (20 percent fat)
Cream, sour	1 cup plain yogurt or 3/4 cup sour milk or buttermilk
Cream, whipping	3/4 cup whole milk plus 1/4 cup butter (30 to 40 percent fat)
Flour, all-purpose	cake flour (add 2 tablespoons for each cup)
Flour, cake	all-purpose flour (subtract 2 tablespoons for each cup)
Flour, self-rising	1¼ teaspoons baking powder plus a pinch of salt for every cup of all-purpose flour
Garlic, small clove	1/2 teaspoon dried minced garlic or 1/8 teaspoon garlic powder
Gingerroot	1/8 teaspoon ground ginger for 1 tablespoon finely chopped gingerroot
Herbs, fresh	1 teaspoon dried herbs for 1 tablespoon finely chopped fresh
Honey	1¼ cups sugar plus 1/3 cup liquid that is required for the recipe
Lemon Juice	1/2 teaspoon white vinegar for each teaspoon
Mustard	1 teaspoon dry mustard for 1 tablespoon mustard
Tomatoes, canned	2½ cups peeled fresh tomatoes (cook for 10 minutes)
Vanilla Bean	1 teaspoon vanilla extract for 1-inch piece

COMMON MEASUREMENTS AND EQUIVALENTS

1 teaspoon	=	1/3 tablespoon or 60 drops
3 teaspoons	=	1 tablespoon
1/2 tablespoon	=	1½ teaspoons
1 tablespoon	=	3 teaspoons or 1/2 fluid ounce
2 tablespoons	=	1/8 cup or 1 fluid ounce
3 tablespoons	=	1½ fluid ounces or 1 jigger
4 tablespoons	=	1/4 cup or 2 fluid ounces
8 tablespoons	=	1/2 cup or 4 fluid ounces
16 tablespoons	=	1 cup, 8 fluid ounces or 1/2 pint
1/8 cup	=	2 tablespoons or 1 fluid ounce
1/4 cup	=	4 tablespoons or 2 fluid ounces
1/3 cup	=	5 tablespoons plus 1 teaspoon
3/8 cup	=	1/4 cup plus 2 tablespoons
1/2 cup	=	8 tablespoons or 4 fluid ounces
2/3 cup	=	10 tablespoons plus 2 teaspoons
5/8 cup	=	1/2 cup plus 2 tablespoons
3/4 cup	=	12 tablespoons or 6 fluid ounces
7/8 cup	=	3/4 cup plus 2 tablespoons
1 cup	=	16 tablespoons, 1/2 pint or 8 fluid ounces
2 cups	=	1 pint or 16 fluid ounces
1 pint	=	2 cups or 16 fluid ounces
1 quart	=	2 pints, 4 cups or 32 fluid ounces
1 gallon	=	4 quarts, 8 pints, 16 cups or 128 fluid ounces

YIELDS AND EQUIVALENTS

Food	Size	Approximate Yield
Apples	1 medium	1 cup chopped
Bananas	1 medium	1 cup sliced
Beans, green	1 pound	3 cups sliced
Berries	1 pint	1¾ cups
Cabbage	1 pound	3½ to 4 cups shredded
Carrots	2 medium	1 cup sliced
	1½ medium	1 cup shredded
Cauliflower	1 pound	3 cups flowerets
Celery	2 medium stalks	1 cup sliced
Corn	2 to 3 medium ears	1 cup kernels
Green pepper	1 medium	1 cup chopped
Lemon Juice	1 medium	3 tablespoons
Lemon Peel	1 medium	2 teaspoons grated
Lettuce	1 pound	6 cups torn pieces
Mushrooms	1/2 pound	3 cups sliced
Onion, green	9 with tops	1 cup sliced
Onion, white	1 medium	1/2 cup chopped
Orange	1 medium	1/3 cup juice
Potatoes	1 medium	1 cup diced
	1 medium	1 cup grated
	1 medium	1 cup sliced

Food	Size	Approximate Yield
Strawberries	1 quart	4 cups sliced
Tomatoes	1 medium	1 cup chopped
	3 medium	1 pound
Yellow Squash	1 medium	1½ cups
Zucchini	1 medium	2 cups sliced

HELPFUL HINTS

FRUITS

To prevent apple slices from browning, toss them in pineapple or lemon juice.

Sprinkle a little lemon juice on banana slices to prevent browning.

To open a coconut, pierce the dark spots with an ice pick. Pour out the coconut milk. Freeze coconut for about one hour; remove from freezer and hit sharply in the middle with hammer.

Rub a slice of kiwi on tough meat. The enzymes in the kiwi will make the meat tender.

Room-temperature lemons yield more juice than chilled ones. If lemons are cold, microwave for 30 seconds on high before juicing. Soak the lemon in hot water for 30 seconds.

To peel peaches, place in boiling water for 30 seconds; remove and place in iced water. The skin comes off easily. To prevent sliced peaches from discoloring, sprinkle with lemon juice.

Never add fresh pineapple or its juice to gelatin because the enzyme bromelain prevents jelling.

To plump raisins, cover raisins with very hot water and soak 2 to 5 minutes. (Do not let raisins soak longer because soaking can result in flavor loss.) Drain well before using. (Raisins in liquid batter do not need to be plumped.)

To make cutting easier, dip kitchen scissors in hot water to cut dried fruit into bite-sized pieces.

▼ ▼ ▼ ▼ ▼ ▼ ▼ ▼ ▼ ▼ ▼ ▼ ▼ ▼ ▼ ▼ ▼ ▼

VEGETABLES

To cook asparagus spears, tie whole stalks in bundles with string and cook upright in 1-inch boiling salted water in deep, narrow pan or a clean coffeepot until stalk ends are crisp-tender, about 7 to 10 minutes.

If broccoli stems are larger than 1-inch thick, cut lengthwise slits for even cooking.

To keep red cabbage from turning purple while cooking, add 2 tablespoons lemon juice or vinegar to cooking water.

To preserve carrots' crispness, remove leafy green tops before storing carrots.

For more tender corn, cook corn in unsalted water with 1 tablespoon sugar and 1 tablespoon lemon juice for each gallon water.

To remove the core from iceberg lettuce easily, strike core end against a flat surface, twist and lift out.

To retain the white color of mushrooms when pan-frying, add 1 teaspoon lemon juice to 1 pound mushrooms.

Clean mushrooms with a soft brush or damp cloth to brush the dirt off, then rinse under cold running water. Do not let them stand in water because they soak up liquid.

Avoid cooking okra in brass, copper or iron; these metals cause discoloration of okra pods.

To sweeten breath after eating onions and garlic, eat several sprigs of parsley that have been dipped in salt or vinegar.

To keep onion whole and keep inner section from slipping out while boiling, cut an "X" about 1/4 inch deep in stem end before cooking.

To keep the white color of pared potatoes before cooking, toss them with a small amount of lemon juice.

Avoid soaking potatoes in cold water for a long period of time to avoid vitamin loss.

To peel tomatoes easily, dip tomatoes into boiling water 30 seconds, then into cold water. Peel with sharp side of knife.

Never refrigerate tomatoes. Refrigeration makes the flesh of the tomato "pulpy" and kills the flavor. Store tomatoes at room temperature.

To speed up ripening of tomatoes, place in brown paper bag.

Do not add salt to green salad until just before serving. Salt wilts and toughens salad greens.

MEATS

When slicing meat or cutting it into chunks, cut the meat against the grain for the most tender results.

To make slicing meat easier, freeze the meat 30 to 40 minutes until meat is no longer soft (but not rock hard) and then slice into strips.

To get steak, chops, etc. well-browned, always make sure the surface is thoroughly dry. This is very important when you marinate meat.

Salt leaches some of the juices from meat, so salt toward the end of the cooking time or after the meat is cooked.

Never tenderize meat by piercing it with a fork because the natural juices will drain out of the holes.

Use a small ice cream scoop to shape uniform meatballs.

Always dampen your hands with cold water before shaping ground meat mixture into loaves, balls etc.

Rub the top of a meat loaf mixture smooth with cold water to minimize cracking.

To keep a ham steak from curling while cooking, cut a few slashes through the fat edges at about 2-inch intervals.

Let roasted meat stand after cooking to give the juices a chance to settle and the meat to firm up for easier carving.

▼ ▼ ▼ ▼ ▼ ▼ ▼ ▼ ▼ ▼ ▼ ▼ ▼ ▼ ▼ ▼ ▼

POULTRY

Always keep poultry refrigerated until ready to cook.

Bacteria on raw poultry can contaminate other food with which it comes in contact; it is very important to always use hot soapy water to thoroughly wash your hands, cutting board and any utensils used.

Remove the skin and any pockets of fat on chicken to avoid extra calories.

Do not salt poultry until after cooking. Salt draws out the juices and will make poultry dry.

White meat cooks slightly more quickly than dark meat; cook dark meat about 5 minutes longer.

Do not leave cooked poultry sitting out at room temperature for more than 2 hours to prevent bacterial growth.

Bottled Italian salad dressing makes an easy, instant marinade for all kinds of poultry.

Do not stuff poultry until just before cooking to prevent bacteria growth.

Stuff poultry three-quarters full to allow for the stuffing to expand during cooking.

A general test for doneness: Juices run clear and the meat near the bone at the thickest part is no longer pink.

PASTA

Do not overcook pasta. Cook pasta the minimum number of minutes directed on the package. The best test for doneness is to bite into a piece. Perfectly cooked pasta should be tender but firm (al dente). Always remember that pasta will continue to cook for a few seconds after it is removed from hot water.

Use about 4 quarts of water per pound of pasta. Make sure the water is boiling rapidly before adding pasta.

Add about 2 tablespoons of vegetable oil to cooking water to keep the pasta from sticking and water from boiling over.

Drain pasta well before adding sauce; excess water clings to the pasta and dilutes the sauce.

Select pasta made with durum wheat (also called semolina); it is preferred because it absorbs less water and has a nice flavor.

When pasta sticks together, gently run hot water over for a few seconds and drain thoroughly.

When preparing pasta to be used in a dish that needs further cooking (like Macaroni and Cheese), reduce the cooking time by a third–the pasta will continue to cook and absorb the liquid in the dish.

Pasta should not be rinsed after cooking unless the pasta is to be used for a cold salad; pasta is best when cooked just before it is to be used.

Fresh pasta or homemade pasta takes less time to cook, about 1 to 3 minutes.

BREAD

Many yeast-bread recipes call for a range of flour amounts; flour absorbs less liquid during hot humid months than in dry weather in which it will have absorbed some of the moisture from the atmosphere.

A slightly-sticky-to-the-touch dough will yield a lighter bread; too much flour creates bread that is dry and dense.

Sweet yeast doughs take longer to rise than those that are savory because sugar over-powers the leavening action and produces slow rising.

Sugar adds flavor and tenderness to bread.

Spray electric mixer dough hooks with vegetable cooking spray to keep the dough from climbing up the hook. This also speeds up cleanup.

Place a damp dish towel under pastry board on which you knead to keep the board from sliding around the counter.

If you knead too much flour into dough, lightly sprinkle it with warm water and grad-ually knead in enough water to make th dough pliable.

Always cool quick breads in pan for 10 minutes before removing from pan to allow the bread to set and to make handling easier.

To mix dry and wet ingredients together in quick breads and muffins, just stir until the dry ingredients are moistened. (Do not worry about small lumps.) To avoid dense, tough bread, do not overmix quick bread batter.

It is normal for quick breads to have a cracked top.

MISCELLANEOUS

When measuring ingredients such as honey, molasses, corn syrup etc., spray a measuring cup with vegetable cooking spray or oil a measuring cup. Every drop will easily slip out.

To save an oversalted soup, add a peeled raw potato and simmer for 10 to 15 minutes. Remove the potato before serving.

Always allow roasts or other large cuts of meat to rest for 10 to 15 minutes after cooking to allow the juices to set and to make slicing the meat easier.

Keep canned broth in the refrigerator; the fat will congeal to lift off the surface easily before use.

When making sauces season with salt and pepper after sauce has been reduced; this helps to prevent overseasoning.

Sift powdered sugar to break up lumps.

Create superfine sugar by processing granulated sugar in food processor until powdery.

For overbeaten whipping cream that threatens to turn buttery, gently whisk in additional cream, 1 tablespoon at a time. Do not beat any more than necessary.

To spread the setting of gelatin mixture, place the bowl that contains the gelatin mixture in a larger bowl of iced water. Stir constantly until mixture is cool and has reached the consistency desired. A gelatin mixture that has set too fast can be resoftened by placing the bowl containing the gelatin mixture in a larger bowl of warm water and stirring until desired consistency.

Index

▼ ▼ ▼ ▼ ▼ ▼ ▼ ▼ ▼ ▼ ▼ ▼ ▼ ▼ ▼ ▼ ▼ ▼ ▼

109
Index

Notes

Notes

Notes

Notes

Notes

Notes